PREP

PREP

The Essential
College Cookbook

KATIE SULLIVAN MORFORD

ROOST BOOKS
BOULDER
2019

Roost Books
An imprint of Shambhala Publications, Inc.
4720 Walnut Street
Boulder, Colorado 80301
roostbooks.com

9 8 7 6 5 4 3 2 1

First Edition
Printed in China

♾ This edition is printed on acid-free paper that meets the
American National Standards Institute Z39.48 Standard.
♻ Shambhala makes every effort to print on recycled paper.
For more information please visit www.shambhala.com.

Roost Books is distributed worldwide by Penguin Random House Inc.,
and its subsidiaries.

Designed by Nami Kurita

Library of Congress Cataloging-in-Publication Data
Names: Morford, Katie Sullivan, author.
Title: Prep: the essential college cookbook / Katie Sullivan Morford.
Description: First edition. | Boulder: Roost Books, [2019] | Includes index.
Identifiers: LCCN 2018015797 | ISBN 9781611806106 (pbk.: alk. paper)
Subjects: LCSH: Quick and easy cooking. | College students—Nutrition. |
College students—Life skills guides. | LCGFT: Cookbooks.
Classification: LCC TX833.5 .M676 2019 | DDC 641.5/12—dc23
LC record available at https://lccn.loc.gov/2018015797

For my parents
who prepped me well, both in
and out of the kitchen

CONTENTS

INTRODUCTION

I'm a mom. Let's just get that out of the way. I've got three teenagers, all of whom have told me not to try to be funny or cool in writing this book. I'll do my best.

When my oldest daughter was about to graduate high school, I started thinking about all the skills that she'd need to function in the world. I went into a panic, realizing everything I'd left out or overlooked.

I knew for a fact that she couldn't change a car tire. And I was pretty sure that she'd never hemmed a pair of pants or unclogged a drain.

What I did know was that she was a decent cook but that she had more to learn. As a culinary professional who cares a lot about food and nutrition, I know that if you're going to eat well you need to be able to cook well. So I wrote *Prep*. It's for her . . . and for my two other kids . . . and now it's for you, too.

SO WHY COOK?

With fast-food places pretty much everywhere and supermarkets packed with thousands of convenience foods, you could completely get through life without ever having to use a mixing bowl or chop an onion. But a whole lifetime of frozen dinners and drive-through burgers? Depressing—especially once you see how gratifying it can be to cook from scratch.

Have you ever made something from start to finish, with your own hands? Maybe it was a Halloween costume when you were ten or a radio you built in middle school, but the end product made you feel the same: proud, excited to show it off. Cooking is like that, only your supplies are things such as butter and flour and your tools are pots and pans.

Best of all? You get to eat what you make.

Here are some of the best reasons to cook:

Homemade food tastes good. If you've ever roasted a hot dog over a campfire or eaten a pile of pancakes right out of a buttered skillet on the stove, you know what I'm talking about. Yes, eating food out of take-out containers can be tasty, but with a bit of practice, nothing will be better than the food you cook in your own kitchen.

It saves money. By and large, cooking at home costs less than eating out. Period. You won't always be under your parents' roof with them paying your food bills, so it'll be handy to know how to shop and cook on a budget when you have to think about things such as covering rent or the electric bill.

It's better for you. Meals cooked at home are almost always better for you—lower in calories, unhealthy fats, sugar, and sodium—than food from restaurants. As a result, the people who eat home-cooked food are less likely to be overweight and more likely to be healthier.

It's better for the environment. All the boxes and bags, paper cups and plastic spoons that come with takeout and convenience foods take a real toll on the environment. Cooking at home leaves a lighter carbon footprint, especially if you bring your own bags when you grocery shop.

It's an instant mood elevator. It may sound dramatic, but it's true. If ever I'm a little down, nothing picks me up faster than getting in front of the stove and making something good to eat for myself or someone else.

You can feed your friends. Whether it's a batch of cupcakes or a pan of mac and cheese, making food for friends is one of the best ways I know to care for the people you like or even love. Yes, you can feed friends with pizza delivery, but consider how much more fun it might be to make your own pizza and maybe a salad to go with it. Invite your pals to pitch in and see for yourself why homemade food is so much better than anything that arrives in a box.

WHAT YOU'LL FIND INSIDE

Prep includes ten different recipe chapters that collectively cover a broad range of culinary know-how:

Eggs	Salads	Snacks and little meals
Grains	Vegetables	Food to share
Pasta	Meat, chicken, and fish	Sweets
Beans		

Each chapter has five recipes, just enough to give you a foundation from which to keep on cooking. This is as much as you need to get started in the kitchen. I don't expect that you'll tackle every last recipe (though go right ahead if you want to). But I really believe that if you cook at least 1 dish from each chapter, you'll develop skills to apply to other recipes like it. For example, make the Genius Spaghetti and Tomato Sauce on page 54 and you might be able to tackle your dad's favorite pasta dish. Or bake the One-Bowl Chocolate Chip Cookies in the Sweets chapter and you'll have no problem knocking out a batch of your grandma's snickerdoodles.

I promise you don't have to know anything about cooking in order to get started. You just have to be willing to try, to expect a few fumbles along the way, and, ultimately, to eat some really good food.

GOOD THINGS TO KNOW

Maybe you've spent every day of your childhood at your parent's side learning the ropes in the kitchen. Or maybe you've never picked up a spatula before today. Either way, this part of the book will arm you with the fundamentals to ease your way into the kitchen. If I had to guess, many of you will skip over this section entirely, preferring to dive right into the recipes. Totally understandable, but at the very least, check out the list of 8 tips below. They will serve you well.

8 TIPS FOR RECIPE SUCCESS

You've got the recipe you want to cook, and you've gathered the ingredients to make it happen. To help along the way, here are 8 ideas for finding success at the stove (including cutting yourself some slack when things don't go as planned):

1. **Get out your gear.** Before you start cooking, read the recipe to check if you have the ingredients and equipment you need so that you don't get halfway through only to realize you've come up short.
2. **Taste as you go.** Don't wait until your dish is finished before you taste. Take little bites along the way, adjusting the salt here, adding a squeeze of lemon there, so that by the time it's done, you've got it just right.
3. **Know that everyone messes up.** Even my brother makes mistakes, and he's a Michelin-star chef with a small empire of restaurants. Trial and error will make you a better cook.
4. **Your hands are your best cooking tools.** Don't be afraid to get them messy. There's no better way to toss vegetables in olive oil, test the doneness of a cake, or knead bread than with the most old-fashioned tool of all—your own hands. Use them.
5. **Make it your own.** Not every recipe must be followed to the letter. That's the beauty of home cooking. If you don't like spicy food, cut the amount of chilies in half. If you're crazy about feta cheese, use twice as much.
6. **Double-check your recipe.** Before you put the cookies into the oven or dress the salad, run your eyes along the recipe, making a mental checklist that nothing was left out.
7. **Don't get hung up on perfection.** We live in the age of Instagram where every tart looks like a snapshot from a Parisian bakery. That's not real

life. Focus on how the food tastes and how you enjoyed cooking it, not that it's camera ready.

8. **When all else fails, there's Google.** This is the upside of cooking in the age of the Internet. Use it. If you come upon a term or an ingredient that you don't know, do a quick Google search. You can find every cooking technique under the sun on YouTube. Problem solved.

TERMS & TECHNIQUES

Reading a recipe is like picking up a new language or learning computer code. Recipes have their own format; cooking has its own terminology. Here are some of the biggies.

Preparing Food

Chop. To cut food into small pieces that are all about the same size, about ¼ to ½ inch. The most common foods you'll chop are likely onions, other vegetables, and fresh herbs. To "roughly chop" means the chop is bigger and less precise.

Dice. To cut into smaller, more precise pieces than a chop. It's a cut I rely on for onions and shallots when I'm using them raw, such as in guacamole and salad dressing.

Mince. To cut into a tiny dice. Think of it as the smallest chop you can get without going completely OCD. It's often used for ingredients with strong flavors that you only need in small doses, such as garlic, fresh ginger, and hot peppers.

Peel. To remove the skins of foods, such as potatoes and carrots, using a vegetable peeler. I also sometimes use a vegetable peeler on Parmesan and chocolate for paper-thin shavings.

Whisk. To use a fork or whisk to blend ingredients together. You can whisk flour, baking soda, and salt before adding it to the liquid batter of a cake, for example, or whisk raw eggs in a bowl before scrambling them in a pan.

Whip/Beat. To use a whisk or electric mixer to vigorously blend ingredients together. If you beat heavy cream, for example, it will turn from a rich liquid into soft clouds in a matter of minutes.

Cooking Food

Bake. To cook food in the oven at a slightly lower temperature than when roasting. Baking is often used for desserts, such as cakes and muffins, and casserole dishes, such as lasagna and mac and cheese.

Boil. To heat liquid, most commonly water, in a pot at a high temperature until bubbles break through the surface. A rolling boil is when the liquid bubbles very aggressively. A gentle boil is when the bubbles are quieter and less frequent.

Braise. To cook food in a covered pot with some liquid, typically at a slow rate. It's often used for meat or chicken and is the technique you'd use to make stew, for example.

Broil. To cook food, often meat or chicken, beneath a broiler. Broilers are a heat source located on the top of most ovens that emits powerful heat down on the food below. It's sometimes used instead of a grill, since you get a similar browning effect as grilling.

Brown. To cook so that the surface turns brown. It's used as a verb, as in "to brown the meat," which typically means putting it in a hot skillet, on a grill, or under a broiler, so the steak, pork, or chicken develops an appealing golden brown color. The goal of browning is usually color and texture, not complete cooking, so often you brown meat on the stove and complete cooking in the oven.

Deep-fry. To heat a pot of oil on the stove to about 350°F and submerge food into the oil until cooked to a crisp. Think donuts, fried chicken, or French fries.

Roast. To cook food in the oven at a high temperature. Roasting is commonly used to cook vegetables, meat, and chicken until browned on the outside and tender inside.

Sauté. To cook food in a skillet, sauté pan, or other shallow pan, usually in butter or oil, while stirring regularly to keep the food moving around the pan. Make sure you heat the oil in the pan first so that the food sizzles when you add it to the pan.

Simmer. To heat liquid at a very gentle boil, with small bubbles. It's often used when cooking pasta sauces and soups.

Steam. To cook food in a small amount of water in a covered pot or pan, ideally with the food suspended above the water in a steaming basket. Used for vegetables, rice, and dumplings.

Stir-fry. To cook food in a wok or large skillet at a high temperature, stirring and turning the food in the pan the entire time until it's done. It's similar to sautéing, but a bit more aggressive.

Measurements

Cooking is part art and part science. The science end of the equation sometimes matters more than others, particularly when it comes to baking. In the early stages of learning to cook, be precise in your measurements. As you get more comfortable in the kitchen, you'll learn where you can fudge things (say, a recipe for pasta sauce) and when sticking with the measurements really matters (say, a recipe for cupcakes). I'm no smarty-pants in math, but the equivalents below are ones I rely on all of the time, so they may be useful to you, too.

3 teaspoons = 1 tablespoon

4 tablespoons = 1/4 cup

16 tablespoons = 1 cup

2 tablespoons = 1 fluid ounce

2 cups = 1 pint

2 pints = 1 quart

4 quarts = 1 gallon

8 fluid ounces = 1 cup

1 stick of butter =
   8 tablespoons = 1/2 cup

ESSENTIAL SKILLS

Getting the hang of things in the kitchen is no different from learning any other skill, be it woodworking or mastering the violin. You need to have the right tools and to know how to use them. Below you'll find a "how-to" on a number of cooking skills that will bring ease to your efforts at the stove.

Knife Know-How

If you've never in your life picked up a sharp knife, find someone who knows what they're doing to show you the basics. Alternatively, look online for video tutorials. The *New York Times, Serious Eats,* and *The Kitchn* are all good resources. If you're a beginner, start with a knife that's not likely to do any harm, say a butter knife, using soft foods, such as a banana, until you've got the hang of it. With practice you can graduate to a small paring knife and then move on to bigger knives and more intricate work. Know that dull knives are more dangerous than sharp ones and all culinary knives should be washed by hand, not in the dishwasher.

How you hold a chef's knife is key to getting the best control when cutting. The ideal grip is to hold firmly to the handle and allow your thumb and index finger to press into the sides of the blade as you cut, being sure they are a safe distance from the sharp edge.

How to Chop an Onion

1. Set an onion on a cutting board.
2. Use one hand to steady the onion and use a chef's knife to cut the onion in half through the stem. Remove the papery skin.
3. Lay the halves cut side down. Aim your knife in the direction of the stem and cut thin rows of slices nearly through to the other side.
4. Cut a row of thin slices in the opposite direction, resulting in a pile of chopped onion.

How to Mince Garlic

1. Set a whole bulb of garlic on a cutting board.
2. Pull a clove off the bulb and use the bottom of a sturdy measuring cup to smash the garlic enough that the skin splits open. Remove the garlic skin.
3. Steady the garlic clove with one hand and use a chef's knife in the other to cut very thin slices.
4. Cut the slices in the opposite direction and then keep chopping until the garlic is in tiny pieces.

How to Cut an Avocado

1. Put an avocado on a cutting board.
2. Steady the avocado with your hand and run a sharp knife lengthwise along the center, cutting around the entire avocado. (There's a big pit in the center, so you won't be able to cut it all the way through.) Hold the 2 sides of the avocado and twist it apart.
3. Dip a small spoon beneath the avocado pit to wedge it out.
4. Dig a large spoon between the skin and the flesh of the avocado, running it along the bottom to scoop out the flesh.

How to Chop Herbs

Basil, mint, and sage. Pull the leaves from the stems and stack them in a pile. Roll up into a tight tube and cut crosswise into very thin slices. If you want them finer, keep chopping until they're done to your liking.

Oregano, rosemary, and thyme. Pull or strip the leaves from the stems. Arrange the leaves in a dense pile and chop with a chef's knife.

Cilantro and parsley. After rinsing the entire bunch under water, give it a good shake and pat it dry with a dish towel. Hold the stem end of the herb bundle in one hand with the bushy tops draped on a cutting board. Use a chef's knife, angled away from you, to shave off as much of the leaves as you need. If you get some stems in the process, not a big deal; they're perfectly edible. Gather the leaves in a dense pile and chop with a chef's knife.

EQUIPMENT

I once heard a well-respected cookbook author say that to make a decent meal, all you need is a sturdy skillet and a fork. Her point was that even though there are thousands of cooking gadgets out there, the tools you really and truly need are very basic.

The Essentials

Baking sheet. (Or better yet, 2 baking sheets.) For baking cookies or roasting vegetables.

Big pot. For cooking pasta, soup, or chili. A 6-quart pot will do. (It should be big enough to fit a football, not that you'll cook a football.)

Can opener. For opening beans, tuna, and other canned foods.

Cheese grater. I prefer a stainless-steel box grater, which has four sides (translation: four options for grating). It sits upright and has a handle at the top.

Colander. For draining pasta and rinsing canned beans. It's useful to have a classic colander with a stable base as well as a fine mesh colander for draining finer ingredients, such as quinoa.

Cutting board. You need at least one and it should be fairly generous in size, maybe as wide across as your shoulders (unless you're a linebacker, in which case, not quite so wide). I prefer wooden boards because I like the way they feel when I'm cutting.

Dish towels. For drying lettuce, hands, and pans, and to use as pot holders.

Instant-read thermometer. To measure the internal temperature of food, such as when your meat or chicken is done.

Knives. You can do nearly everything in the kitchen with 3 basic knives:

1. **Chef's knife.** The workhorse of the kitchen for most cutting jobs, including chopping onions and slicing meat.

2. **Paring knife.** For smaller jobs, such as cutting apples or slicing strawberries.
3. **Serrated-edge knife.** For cutting bread and delicate foods, such as tomatoes.

Large metal spoon. For spooning up foods from pots and pans onto your plate.

Large mixing bowl. For making cake batter or tossing salads. I prefer stainless steel, glass, or ceramic to plastic.

Measuring cups. ¼-, ⅓-, ½-, and 1-cup measures are essential; ⅛ cup and ¾ cup are a bonus.

Measuring spoons. ¼ teaspoon ½ teaspoon, 1 teaspoon, and 1 tablespoon are essential; I also like ⅛ teaspoon and ½ tablespoon.

Pot holders. A pair of these will protect your hands when lifting hot pans.

Rubber spatula. To scrape up every last scrap of brownie batter or cookie dough.

Salad spinner. Not an absolute necessity, but it takes so much of the work out of cleaning and drying lettuce that I put it in the essentials category.

Sauté pan/skillet. For sautéing vegetables, scrambling eggs, browning meat, and so much more. If you were to choose just one pan, go for a cast-iron one that's about 10 inches in diameter. It will last a lifetime, and you can cook practically anything in it (even a cake).

Spatula. For lifting food. A spatula is essential for cooking tasks such as turning over fried eggs, flipping burgers on a grill, or lifting brownies out of a baking pan. I prefer metal spatulas to plastic or silicone.

Vegetable peeler. For peeling carrots and potatoes, and shaving Parmesan and chocolate.

Whisk. For beating eggs and heavy cream.

Wooden spoon. For stirring everything from pancake batter to pasta sauce. It doesn't conduct heat like a metal spoon, so it won't get hot (but it is wood, so keep it away from the flame of your stove).

2- to 3-quart saucepan. Different from a sauté pan/skillet, this is a

small, deep pot good for warming soup, cooking small batches of rice or oatmeal, and boiling eggs.

Nice-to-Haves

Blender. If you like smoothies, this is a must; also good for blending soups, such as the Creamy Black Bean Soup on page 78.

Electric kettle. One of my favorite electric appliances of all time. It boils water in a snap, so you can make a quick cup of tea, instant oatmeal, or noodle soup. It's terrific in a dorm room or first apartment.

Electric mixer. Yes, you can stir cookie dough and cake batter without one, but an electric mixer makes these tasks so much quicker and easier.

Glass measuring cup. Good for measuring liquids, such as milk or water, because it's more precise than a cup measure and has a lip for pouring, like a water pitcher.

Metal tongs. For turning over meat or chicken in a skillet, tossing salad, and cooking food on a grill.

Muffin tin. (Even better, 2 muffin tins.) For making muffins, cupcakes, and single-serve versions of things, such as mac and cheese and meatloaf.

Small sauté pan. For cooking smaller amounts of food, such as a single quesadilla or an omelet. Look for something that's about 6 to 8 inches across.

Toaster oven. More energy efficient than turning on a whole oven and capable of cooking so much more than toast, such as small batches of cookies, vegetables, or a chicken breast.

Two 8- or 9-inch round cake pans. For making birthday cakes.

9 x 5-inch loaf pan. For baking quick breads, such as the Golden Banana Bread on page 162, cakes, and meatloaf.

9 x 13-inch glass or metal baking dish. For making lasagna, casseroles, mac and cheese, brownies, and single-layer cakes.

Bells and Whistles

Food processor. Does everything from grate cheese to mix bread dough to shred vegetables in seconds.

Handheld citrus juicer. Makes very easy work of getting every last drop of juice out of lemons, limes, and other citrus fruits.

Ice cream scoop. Ice cream junkies would argue that this should go in the essentials category.

Kitchen scissors. (Sometimes called kitchen shears.) Good for quickly snipping herbs instead of chopping them with a knife or for cutting through chicken bones.

Pizza stone. Makes for a really crispy pizza crust.

Roasting pan with sides. Even though you can do plenty of roasting jobs in a baking pan or a large baking sheet, a proper roasting pan will serve you well.

Rolling pin. For rolling out pie dough or sugar cookies. If you don't have one, you can use a large glass water bottle.

Silicone baking mat. A thin piece of silicone that you can use in place of nonstick spray, foil, or parchment paper when you don't want food to stick to a baking sheet. (Silpat is a common brand.)

Stand-up mixer. It beats batter quickly and efficiently and has attachments that knead bread dough and grind meat.

Waffle iron. For waffles, of course, but it can also double as a panini press.

INGREDIENTS

When it comes to cooking, ingredients matter. A juicy ripe tomato that you buy in season makes an entirely different pasta sauce than one picked in January and shipped across the continent. Here are some thoughts on a handful of staple ingredients that you will cook with again and again.

Black pepper. When adding pepper to food, I typically use a pepper grinder, which grinds the pepper fresh and lends a bigger pop of flavor than preground pepper. That said, this is an extra step for cooks-in-training, so feel free to rely on ground pepper as you see fit until you get the hang of things.

Butter. Butter is sold both salted and unsalted. I almost always cook with salted butter, so unless a recipe calls out "unsalted," assume you should use salted. Don't substitute margarine for butter. It just doesn't taste as good, and there is a huge range in quality, nutritional value, and how it will work (or not work) in a recipe.

Kosher salt. I always have about a cup of kosher salt in a covered container near the stove in my kitchen. It's coarser and less metallic tasting than common iodized salt. When I'm cooking, I'll grab a pinch of salt to add to eggs, dip in a measuring spoon when I need salt for baking, or scoop up a small handful to season a pot of pasta water. I recommend you ditch the salt shaker and do the same. Over time you'll get a feel for just how much you need.

Milk and yogurt. Milk and yogurt are made with a variety of fat contents, from nonfat to whole. For most of the recipes, I don't specify the fat content; I leave it up to you, depending on what you have on hand. Just know that the higher the fat content, the richer and creamier the milk or yogurt will be (which means higher calories, too). Also worth noting, these recipes were developed using cow's milk. Therefore I can't vouch for how the recipes will measure up if made with soy, almond, or other milk. Generally speaking, smoothies, grains, and egg dishes work well using plant-based milks, as long as you use an unflavored and unsweetened variety.

Olive oil. The great majority of the oil I use in cooking is olive oil. I always have a bottle within reach, and it's always extra-virgin oil. Even though it's more expensive than plain olive oil, it's the best tasting and the best for you. Be sure to store all of your oil in a cool dark place, such as a cupboard that isn't too close to a heat source.

Parmesan cheese. A block of Parmesan is a permanent fixture in my fridge. I prefer the one labeled Parmigiano-Reggiano, which is the cream of the crop. Whatever kind you buy, it's usually best to buy a whole piece and grate it yourself rather than buying it pregrated (unless it's from a good Italian deli where they grate it on the spot). Don't buy the grated Parmesan sold in the green plastic container, which is of criminally poor quality and shouldn't be allowed to bear the Parmesan label.

Groceries

It's possible to pull together a very good meal with very few ingredients. Here is a list of the staples I try to have on hand for cooking, filling in with fresh foods—fruits, vegetables, chicken, or fish—as needed for a specific recipe.

Pantry

Extra-virgin olive oil

Canola oil or another vegetable oil (I buy expeller-pressed organic canola oil)

Kosher salt

Black pepper

A few vinegars, such as balsamic, red wine, white wine, apple cider, and/or rice vinegar

Soy sauce

Assorted dry herbs and spices, such as paprika, cumin, coriander, oregano, and cinnamon

Onions

Garlic

Lemons

Pasta

Grains, such as rice and oatmeal

Basic baking ingredients: flour, sugar, brown sugar, baking soda, baking powder, vanilla

Canned tomatoes

Dried and canned beans

Nuts and seeds

Fridge

Eggs

Milk

Plain Greek or regular yogurt (sometimes both)

Butter

Ketchup

Dijon mustard

Mexican salsa

Parmesan cheese

Another favorite cheese, such as Cheddar or Monterey Jack

Carrots

Celery

Hot pepper sauce, such as sriracha

Lettuce/leafy greens

Freezer

A variety of fruits

Corn

Chopped spinach

Peas

Ice

Ground turkey or beef

Bacon

SAFETY

Since cooking involves heat and raw meat, it's wise to know some safety basics.

Hot Stuff

Any heat source in the kitchen calls for extra attention. Here are some quick tips for keeping you and your kitchen safe:

- Turn pan handles parallel to the front edge of the stove. You're less likely to knock into a handle and cause a hot pan to go flying.
- Have good pot holders or sturdy dish towels within reach to pull dishes from the oven and hold on to pan handles. Never use a pot holder or dish towel that's damp, since the heat can sear right through.
- Keep cloth and paper towels away from the heat source to avoid going up in flames.
- Know where your fire extinguisher is and how to use it.
- Don't put anything plastic near, on, or in the stove or oven.
- Turn off the stove or oven when you're done. I've learned the hard way that if you don't do it as soon as your dish is finished, you often forget.

Food Safety

We've got to hand it to modern technology for giving us refrigerators, freezers, antibacterial soap, plastic wrap, and glass storage containers to help prevent food poisoning. All food, no matter how clean it is, has small amounts of potentially harmful bacteria. The key to keeping food safe is to prevent the bacteria from multiplying to a level that might make you sick, as well as avoid transferring bacteria from one food to another. Here are a few food safety pointers that may come in handy:

Wash your hands. Something you've probably been told your whole life, but it's good advice. A good soapy handwashing before and after cooking is your best armor against food poisoning.

Keep cold food cold. Any perishable food should get a little extra TLC in the kitchen. If it was refrigerated or frozen at the supermarket, be sure to store it that way at home.

Keep hot food hot. Once food is cooked, it should be kept hot until ready to serve or cooled and kept in the fridge. For example, let's say you make a pot of turkey chili at noon and your friends aren't coming until 8:00 p.m. Transfer it to a bowl or container and put it in the fridge to cool. Then transfer it back to the pot to reheat on the stove when it's time to eat.

Take extra care with meat, chicken, and fish. Think of raw meat, chicken, and fish as loners. That is, it's best to keep them separate from other foods or cooking tools that are in contact with other ingredients. If you cut raw chicken on a cutting board, for example, you need to give the board, knife, your hands, and any surface the chicken has touched a hot and soapy scrub before you go on to make a salad or slice a melon.

Cleanup

Cleaning up the mess is the only real downside of cooking as far as I'm concerned. I'm not particularly good at it, but because I spend so much time in the kitchen I've learned a few tricks that make it less overwhelming once the cooking is done:

Start with a clean kitchen. Yes, it's a drag to have to clean up before you even begin in the kitchen, but your cooking will feel less chaotic if your space is tidy.

Clean as you go. As much as possible, clean up a little bit all along the way as you cook. If you dirty a cutting board while chopping an onion, for example, wash it and put it away while you're sautéing the onion.

Make a deal. In our house, the person who does the cooking doesn't have to do the dishes.

So now that you know some of the basics, the fun part begins: cooking. Start by choosing a recipe that grabs your eye, something you really want to eat. Write down the ingredients you need and stock up at the market. When the time comes to cook, don't rush it. Ideally cooking isn't just a means to an end—good food—but an enjoyable endeavor in and of itself. Bon appétit.

1 PREP EGGS LIKE A PRO

Eggs are like no other ingredient on the planet. Whether poached, fried, or boiled, eggs are the foundation for excellent, affordable, healthy meals. Housed inside that delicate shell is a key ingredient for so many favorite recipes. They scramble up into fluffy eggs, help cakes rise, and lend creaminess to chocolate custard. You can pick up a whole carton for just a few bucks and then turn it into a week of breakfasts or a single meal to feed all your friends.

Eggs are good for you, too. A single egg has a weensy 70 calories and is packed with nutrients. They're immensely versatile, too. If ever I'm down to just a few ingredients in my fridge but need to make dinner, an egg is often what I grab.

SOFTLY SCRAMBLED EGGS

Scrambled eggs may seem like a breeze to make, but they're often not done very well. They're routinely cooked too aggressively at too high a heat and so are rubbery and overdone. Be gentle with your eggs, keeping the heat to medium and scrambling them just enough. Turn off the stove before they look quite done, since the heat of the pan alone will finish the cooking for you.

2 eggs

2 tablespoons milk

1 teaspoon butter

Salt and black pepper

KEY EQUIPMENT: small bowl, medium skillet (ideally nonstick or cast-iron), rubber spatula

PRO TIP: You can easily multiply the recipe to feed more people. Just be sure to use a big enough pan with a nice slick of butter along the bottom and know that the cooking time may be a little longer.

Crack the eggs into a small bowl and add the milk. Use a fork to vigorously whisk the eggs until they're an even yellow color.

Put a medium skillet on the stove over medium heat. When the pan is hot, add the butter and let it melt, tilting the pan this way and that so the butter coats the entire bottom.

Add the eggs and let them spread out. Don't touch the pan for 30 seconds. Use a rubber spatula to gently push the eggs from the edge of the pan to the middle, allowing raw egg to drift back out to the edge. Continue to turn the eggs in the pan several times until they look nearly cooked. Remove from heat, stir again once or twice, by which time the eggs should be just cooked. The whole operation takes about 1 minute.

Transfer eggs to a plate and sprinkle a pinch of salt and freshly ground black pepper over the surface. Taste, and add more if desired.

How to Crack an Egg

Hold the egg in the fingers of your dominant hand as if you've got a tennis ball. Gently tap the egg a time or two on the edge of a bowl until you crack the shell. Lift the egg over the bowl and dig your thumbs into the crack. Open the shell, breaking it in half, and allow the egg to fall into the bowl. If a piece of egg shell lands in the bowl, dip another piece of shell next to it. It acts like a magnet and will help remove the wayward shell.

DOUBLE-CINNAMON FRENCH TOAST

French toast is one of those clever dishes invented as a way to use up stale bread. When bread is past its prime, home cooks soak it in milk and eggs and cook it on a hot griddle. You can get that same stale effect by toasting cinnamon-raisin bread very briefly before dipping it in egg batter. It gets moist without going soggy and browns up beautifully in melted butter.

6 slices cinnamon-raisin bread

2 eggs

½ cup milk

1 teaspoon ground cinnamon

1 teaspoon vanilla extract

1 tablespoon butter, divided

Pure maple syrup or jam for serving

KEY EQUIPMENT: medium bowl, large skillet, spatula, toaster

PRO TIP: Make a double batch and put leftover slices in a freezer bag. Store in the refrigerator for a few days or in the freezer for up to a month. Reheat slices in the toaster.

Toast the bread just enough so that it feels slightly stale but not at all browned. Remove from toaster.

Crack the eggs into a medium bowl. Add the milk, cinnamon, and vanilla and use a fork or whisk to beat the ingredients together until an even color.

Put the egg mixture and toasted bread next to the stove.

Put a large skillet on the stove over medium-high heat. When the pan is hot, add half the butter and tilt the pan so the butter coats the bottom.

Plunge a slice of bread into the egg mixture, immersing it and turning it for about 10 seconds so both sides soak up the liquid. Remove from egg mixture and quickly place in the hot pan. Continue with as many more bread slices as will fit in 1 layer in the pan. Cook the French toast slices on one side until deeply browned. Use a spatula to turn them over to brown the other side. When done, transfer to a large plate. Melt the remaining butter in the pan and continue with any remaining bread slices.

Serve warm with maple syrup or jam.

What's with All the Different Eggs?

The next time you're at the supermarket, check out the egg section. The variety of options is sort of mind-blowing—free-range, cage-free, pastured, pasteurized, organic, omega-3, brown eggs, white eggs, jumbo, and so on. Here's the skinny:

Large eggs are the standard. All the recipes in this book (and in most cookbooks) were developed using large eggs, so that's your best bet.

Color doesn't matter. Most eggs are white, plenty are brown, and some are even pale blue. The color of the shell is just an indication of the breed of chicken from which it was laid.

Cost varies a lot. A carton of eggs can go for as little as one dollar a dozen to over ten dollars for very special eggs at very fancy markets. Organic eggs—which means the chickens were given feed grown without pesticides, not given antibiotics, and were required to have a certain amount and type of space to roam—tend to be on the pricier end of the spectrum.

Farmers' markets are good places to buy eggs. The best eggs I've tasted have come from roadside farm stands or farmers' markets. The chickens that lay these eggs often get to wander around freely and snack on their natural environment. The result is often a very rich yolk and flavorful egg. Try them sometime and see for yourself.

OVER EASY FRIED EGG SANDWICH

MAKES 1 SERVING

The only time my parents ever took us to McDonald's when I was a kid was for breakfast on road trips. I always ordered the same thing: an Egg McMuffin. This is a homemade version that is seriously better than the original. Everything is done in one pan, so it's easy cleanup, too. If you don't like fried eggs, you can make this with scrambled eggs instead.

Nonstick cooking spray

1 egg

1 slice ham

1 small handful baby spinach (¼ cup)

1 thin slice Cheddar cheese (about the size of an English muffin)

1 English muffin

KEY EQUIPMENT: medium skillet (ideally nonstick or cast-iron), spatula, toaster

PRO TIP: Don't like spinach? Use a slice of tomato instead.

Spray a light coating of nonstick cooking spray over the surface of a medium skillet. Set the pan on the stove over medium-high heat. When the pan is good and hot, crack the egg onto one side of the pan. Place the ham on the other side of the pan. Cover the ham with the spinach, followed by the cheese, all in a little stack.

Meanwhile, toast the English muffin until lightly browned around the edges.

When the white of the egg is fairly firm with a little color along the bottom, about 1 to 1½ minutes, turn it over with a spatula. After 30 seconds or so, when the other side is firm but the yolk is still soft, remove pan from heat. Use a spatula to transfer the ham-spinach-cheese stack on top of an English muffin half. Transfer the egg on top of the ham (you may need to fold in the edges of everything so it doesn't drape too much over the muffin). Cover with remaining muffin half. Serve immediately.

The Yolk Is Where It's At

As a kid, I only liked egg whites. I carefully ate around the oozing yolk of the fried eggs on my breakfast plate. Eventually I learned to like (and now I love) the whole egg. And it's a good thing, since the yolks are what give eggs their richness and flavor. The yolk is also home to most of the vitamins and minerals.

Egg Storage 101

- Store eggs in the fridge, where they will keep for about 3 weeks.
- If you hard-boil eggs, store them in the fridge for up to 1 week.
- If you crack an egg into a bowl but don't use it, you can refrigerate it for up to 3 days.
- When you pick up a carton of eggs at the store, open it and have a peek to make sure none of the shells are cracked before you buy.
- If you have egg whites left over from a recipe, you can freeze them in a covered container for next time.

HARD-BOILED EGGS

What I like about hard-boiled eggs is that you can cook several at once to keep in your fridge and use throughout the week. Grab one and sprinkle it with salt and pepper to eat for a quick breakfast or snack. Or peel a few for egg salad sandwiches, deviled eggs, or to slice onto a salad.

4 eggs

KEY EQUIPMENT: medium saucepan with lid

PRO TIP: The freshest eggs are the hardest to peel. It's better to use eggs that have been in your fridge for a week or more for hard-boiling; they will be easier to peel when the time comes.

Put the eggs in a medium saucepan and fill with enough water to cover the eggs by 1 inch. Put the pot on the stove over high heat. Bring the water to a boil. Once it boils, cover the pot with a lid, turn off the heat, and right away, set a timer for 12 minutes. When the timer rings, use a large spoon to lift the eggs from the pot.

Store in the refrigerator, where they will keep for up to 1 week, or tap on the counter, peel, and eat.

Did You Know?

You can tell a raw egg from a hard-boiled one by spinning it on the counter. The hard-boiled egg will spin rapidly and the raw one will be more sluggish and a little wobbly.

CHEESE OMELET

When I tried my first French omelet, it was nothing like what I'd eaten in American diners, which tend to be supersized and packed with ingredients. Instead it was delicate, filled with just cheese, and melt-in-your-mouth tender. Considering that omelets have a long history in France, it's no wonder they know what they're doing. Hopefully you'll like it just as much as I did.

2 eggs

⅛ teaspoon salt

Freshly ground black pepper

½ tablespoon butter

¼ cup grated Cheddar or Gruyere cheese

KEY EQUIPMENT: small bowl, 8- to 10-inch sauté pan (ideally nonstick), rubber spatula, cheese grater

PRO TIP: Feel free to add a few tablespoons of one of the following fillings along with the cheese: chopped ham, chopped spinach, crumbled bacon, or sliced sautéed mushrooms.

Crack the eggs into a small bowl, add salt and black pepper—a few turns will do. Use a fork to vigorously whisk the eggs until they are an even yellow color.

Set an 8- to 10-inch sauté pan over medium heat. Add the butter and let it melt, tilting the pan so it coats the entire bottom and up the sides a bit.

When the pan is hot, pour in the eggs and let them settle for 10 seconds until the bottom cooks a bit. Using a rubber spatula, stir the eggs in the pan a few times. Then let the eggs settle, tilting the pan to help the raw parts spread to the edges. Use a rubber spatula to lift the edge of the omelet in one spot and tilt the pan so the liquid parts drift into the bare spot and set. Do this in 4 or 5 places around the perimeter of the omelet until the top is nearly cooked. Sprinkle the cheese over the eggs and remove from heat. If the eggs don't look quite done and the cheese needs to melt a little longer, put a lid over the pan for about 30 seconds.

Use a rubber spatula to lift one edge of the omelet and roll it up in the pan with the cheese tucked inside. Lift the pan off the stove, tilt it, and slide the omelet onto a plate.

Serve immediately.

Choose Your Own Adventure:
EGG SCRAMBLE YOUR WAY

Think of an egg scramble as a deconstructed omelet. Instead of the cheese and other fillings being folded inside the egg, everything gets scrambled together into a delicious mess.

Crack 2 eggs into a small bowl and whisk with a fork. Cook in a pan using the Softly Scrambled method on page 26.

When the eggs are nearly cooked, add ¼ cup of any of the following:
- chopped cooked potatoes, zucchini, mushrooms, or broccoli and/or raw baby spinach, baby kale, or diced tomatoes
- 2 tablespoons chopped ham, crumbled cooked bacon, diced cooked sausage, or chopped Canadian bacon

- 2 to 3 tablespoons grated Cheddar, Monterey Jack, or Swiss cheese, or crumbled feta or goat cheese

Gently scramble everything together in the pan, season with salt and pepper, and transfer to a plate.

2 MAKE OATMEAL, RICE, AND OTHER GRAINS

Grains are an essential ingredient in hundreds of foods we eat every day. The wheat in your sandwich bread? A grain. The rice that comes with your teriyaki takeout? Also a grain. Ditto for the oats in your morning oatmeal. Grains are a huge part of diets the world over. Think about, for example, how important rice is in places such as China, Japan, and India, or how important millet is in parts of Africa. There's no doubt that grains are popular, and for good reason:

They're cheap. Whether it's cornmeal or quinoa, just a few dollars can buy enough grains to get you through several meals. It's one of the reasons grains make so much sense for young people who may not have the budget for expensive groceries.

They taste good. Grains are like a blank piece of paper before you start to paint: plain. Add just a little of this or that—a pat of butter, a spoonful of Parmesan cheese, or a splash of soy sauce—and you've got the beginning of something good.

They're versatile. Cook a pot of grains and you can find 10 different ways to turn it into a meal. Rice, for example, can be made into fried rice, or stirred into a sweet pudding, or rolled up like sushi.

They're nutritious. Grains are filling and good for you, especially if you choose less-processed grains, otherwise known as "whole" grains. Examples include whole wheat bread, brown rice, and rolled oats.

BROWN SUGAR-CINNAMON OATMEAL

In a matter of minutes, you can whip up a bowl of oatmeal to help a hunger fix any time of day. While it's cooking, pull out your favorite toppings. Brown sugar and raisins are pretty standard, but you can experiment with maple syrup, nuts, seeds, or any fresh or dried fruit.

1¾ cups water

1 cup old-fashioned rolled oats (not quick oats)

⅛ teaspoon kosher salt

¼ teaspoon ground cinnamon

⅓ cup milk

2 thin slices butter (about 2 teaspoons)

2 teaspoons brown sugar

Toppings (optional): raisins, chopped nuts, hemp seeds, dried cranberries, chopped dried apple, berries, or sliced banana

KEY EQUIPMENT:
medium saucepan

Put the water, oats, salt, and cinnamon into a medium saucepan and set on the stove over high heat. When tiny bubbles appear around the entire edge of the pot, stir in the milk. Let it come to a gentle boil. Stir and drop the heat down enough so the oatmeal bubbles just a little. Cook, stirring it from time to time, until the oatmeal is tender and creamy, about 5 minutes from when you added the milk. Remove from heat.

Transfer to 2 serving bowls. Top each bowl with a thin slice of butter, the brown sugar, and any favorite toppings. Add more milk if the oatmeal is too thick.

PRO TIP: Try oatmeal savory instead of sweet. Rather than brown sugar and cinnamon, top it with grated cheese, a fried egg, or just fresh black pepper. You eat other grains this way, so why not oats?

How to Make Your Own Microwave Oatmeal

Instead of buying little packets of microwave oatmeal, you can make your own. Here's how: Put ⅓ cup old-fashioned rolled oats and ⅔ cup water in a deep glass or ceramic cereal bowl (big enough that the oatmeal doesn't overflow as it cooks). Stir, then cook in the microwave on high until the oatmeal is tender and has absorbed most of the water, about 2 minutes. Stir again and add milk and any favorite toppings.

Did You Know?

Oatmeal is a real superfood. It's been used for decades to help lower "bad" cholesterol and boost "good" cholesterol.

SO EASY COUSCOUS

Couscous is teeny tiny in size, made from wheat, and common in parts of North Africa and the Middle East. This might make it sound exotic, but the taste is mild and it couldn't be easier to cook. Unlike so many other grains that take a while, couscous is nearly instantaneous, coming together so quickly that it feels a little like magic.

1¼ cups water

1 teaspoon plus 1 tablespoon extra-virgin olive oil, divided

¾ teaspoon kosher salt

1 cup couscous

2 green onions

¼ teaspoon ground coriander

⅓ cup raisins

¼ cup slivered almonds

KEY EQUIPMENT: small saucepan with a lid, cutting board, chef's knife

PRO TIP: This is best with toasted almonds, which you can make by spreading them on a baking sheet and baking them in a preheated 350°F oven until golden brown, about 7 minutes. Keep an eye on them, so you don't end up with a pan of burned nuts.

Combine the water, 1 teaspoon of the olive oil, and the salt in a small saucepan. Set on the stove over high heat and cook until it boils. Add the couscous, stir once, put on the lid, and remove from heat. Set a timer for 4 minutes.

Lay the green onions on a cutting board. Trim off the hairy-looking tips and dark green parts and discard. Slice the white and light green parts very thin.

Lift the lid and use a fork to scrape along the couscous (a little like raking leaves) until it breaks up into a fluffy pile. Add the remaining 1 tablespoon of olive oil, green onions, coriander, and raisins. Stir well. Scatter the almonds over the top and serve.

SERVE WITH: Maple-Mustard Pork Chops on page 125.

SIZZLING FRIED RICE

My favorite time of day to eat fried rice is in the morning. Maybe that's because it has eggs in it, which I consider a breakfast food. Of course, it's good for lunch or dinner, too, and it's excellent reheated and eaten the next day.

4 green onions

1 medium clove garlic

2 eggs

1 tablespoon canola oil or other vegetable oil

3 cups cooked brown rice (see Easy Brown Rice, below)

½ cup chopped ham

½ cup frozen peas (run under warm water in a colander to defrost; drain)

1 large handful baby spinach

1 teaspoon toasted sesame oil (substitute canola oil if you don't have sesame oil)

1 tablespoon seasoned rice vinegar

1 teaspoon soy sauce

¼ teaspoon kosher salt

Sriracha or other hot pepper sauce (optional)

KEY EQUIPMENT: cutting board, chef's knife, small bowl, large skillet or wok, wooden spoon

Lay the green onions on a cutting board. Trim off the hairy-looking tips and dark green ends and discard. Cut the remaining white and light green parts into very thin slices. Mince the garlic.

Crack the eggs into a small bowl and use a fork to whisk them until blended and an even color.

Pour the canola oil into a large skillet or wok set on the stove over medium heat. When the pan is hot, add the green onions and garlic and sauté, stirring everything in the pan with a wooden spoon for 30 seconds. Turn the heat to high and add the rice, stir, and spread it across the pan. Leave for 1 minute to crisp the rice. Add the ham, peas, and spinach, and stir again.

Push the rice far over to one side of the skillet. In the empty part of the pan, add the sesame oil and pour the eggs into the oil. Stir the eggs in the pan several times until just cooked through, then gently mix the eggs into the rice. Add the rice vinegar, soy sauce, and salt, and mix well.

Remove from heat and serve with sriracha or other hot pepper sauce on the side, if desired.

Easy Brown Rice

The most foolproof method for cooking rice is to boil it the same way you cook pasta. Here's how: Put 8 cups of water, 1½ teaspoons kosher salt, and 2 bay leaves into a medium pot and put on the stove over high heat. Bring it to a boil, add 1 cup long-grain brown rice, and stir. Boil the rice, uncovered, until tender but not mushy, about 40 minutes. To test for doneness, use a spoon to scoop up a few grains to taste. If it's tender without any crunch, it's done. Set a colander in the sink, pour in the rice, and leave it to drain for 1 to 2 minutes. Transfer to a bowl and serve with a slice of butter, a splash of soy sauce, or use it to make the Sizzling Fried Rice on page 43. Makes 3¼ cups.

10 Favorite Grains

I suppose like any type of food, there are some grains I love and some I could live without. Here are 10 favorites:

Barley. Good for adding to soups or for grain salads.

Bulgur. The main ingredient in a popular Middle Eastern dish called tabbouleh.

Buckwheat. Buckwheat flour is great in pancakes and baked goods. Whole buckwheat, sometimes called kasha, can be used to make granola and hot cereal.

Cornmeal/polenta. Ground, dried corn sold in a range of textures from fine to course. Used for cornmeal muffins as well as the Cheesy Parmesan Polenta on page 47.

Farro. Makes terrific grain salads and can also be cooked like risotto.

Millet. A good one to add to granola bars and muffins.

Oats. For oatmeal (see recipe, page 40), of course, as well as cookies and granola. Of the three common varieties—rolled, quick-cooking, and steel cut— I find rolled oats to be the most versatile.

Quinoa. I like it warm for breakfast and mixed with pesto as a side dish (see recipe, page 49).

Rice. For sushi, rice pudding, fried rice (see recipe, page 43), curries, and so much more.

Wheat. A buttered slice of whole wheat toast is one of my favorite foods.

CHEESY PARMESAN POLENTA

MAKES 4 SERVINGS AS PART OF A MAIN DISH, 6 SERVINGS AS A SIDE

Warm and creamy, this polenta is real comfort food, much like mashed potatoes and mac and cheese. If you've never had polenta before, it's basically the Italian version of cornmeal grits. You cook it in milk and water until creamy and then finish it with lots of Parmesan cheese. If it thickens too much as it cools, just add a little water or milk and stir well.

1½ cups water

2 cups milk

1 teaspoon kosher salt

⅔ cup polenta, or medium-grain cornmeal

1 tablespoon butter

½ cup finely grated Parmesan cheese, plus more for serving

Freshly ground black pepper

KEY EQUIPMENT: medium saucepan, whisk, cheese grater

PRO TIP: If you have leftover polenta, you can press it into a pan in a 1-inch-thick layer and refrigerate. Once chilled, it's firm enough to cut into squares and brown in a greased skillet over medium-high heat. Eat it with fried eggs for breakfast.

Put the water, milk, and salt in a medium saucepan. Set on the stove over medium-high heat. Cook until the liquid looks like it's just about to boil (keep an eye on it, so it doesn't reach a full boil and spill over the edge of the pot). Slowly add the polenta to the pot with one hand while stirring with a whisk with the other hand. Once the polenta is added, lower the heat until it simmers gently (lightly bubbles). Cook, stirring it frequently, until the polenta absorbs the liquid and is tender, about 25 minutes.

Remove polenta from the heat. Add the butter and Parmesan, stirring until it melts. The polenta will thicken as it cools. You can always thin it by stirring in a little more milk or water, if desired.

Spoon the polenta into serving bowls and add a little freshly ground black pepper. Serve immediately with more Parmesan to pass at the table.

SERVE WITH: Garlicky Greens on page 109 or make a double batch of polenta to serve with Homemade Saucy Meatballs on page 152.

PESTO QUINOA

If you're not familiar with quinoa, let's start with the name. It comes from South America and is pronounced KEEN-wah. Even though it's a tiny grain, it's a bit of a powerhouse as far as nutrition goes and is particularly high in protein. Its small size also means it cooks up quickly.

1 cup quinoa

¼ cup basil pesto, either store-bought or homemade (page 64)

1 tablespoon extra-virgin olive oil

Salt to taste

½ lemon

¼ cup toasted pistachios or roughly chopped walnuts

KEY EQUIPMENT: medium saucepan, fine-mesh colander, medium bowl

PRO TIP: Quinoa can be used in many of the same ways you'd use other grains. Serve it as a side dish to chicken or vegetables, or add it to soup or salad.

Put the quinoa into a medium saucepan and add enough water so that the quinoa is covered by at least 1½ inches. Set the pot on the stove over high heat and bring to a boil. When the water boils, drop the heat to medium-high until it quiets down to a gentle boil. Set a timer for 15 minutes. When the timer rings, taste the quinoa to be sure it's done. It should be chewy and tender, not crunchy.

Set a fine-mesh colander in the sink. Empty the quinoa into the colander and rinse briefly under water. Drain for a few minutes.

Transfer the quinoa to a medium bowl. Add the pesto, olive oil, and salt. Squeeze enough lemon juice to measure 2 teaspoons. Add the juice to the quinoa and stir well. Scatter the nuts over the top. Serve warm.

SERVE WITH: The Lemon-Garlic Chicken Thighs on page 118, the Maple-Mustard Pork Chops on page 125, or the Chopped Greek Salad on page 89.

Did You Know?

Even though it looks and tastes like a grain, quinoa is actually a seed. It's considered a pseudocereal.

Choose Your Own Adventure:
COLORFUL GRAIN BOWLS

If you have a bowl of cooked grains tucked away in your fridge, it can easily be turned into a super-quick meal with just a few extra ingredients. The ratio of grains to fixings varies, but figure 1 cup cooked grains to ⅓ cup to ⅔ cup fixings.

Choose a grain
quinoa, rice, farro, barley, sorghum, polenta, couscous, or freekeh
+
Add a drizzle of olive and pinch of salt and pepper
+
Top with favorite fixings, such as
- cherry tomatoes + little mozzarella balls + chopped basil
- black beans + corn + chopped cilantro
- stir-fried veggies + teriyaki sauce + toasted peanuts
- rice vinegar + cooked edamame + sliced green onions
- chopped olives + chopped parsley + feta cheese
- crispy bacon bits + baby spinach + avocado
- pesto + chopped walnuts + cooked broccoli
- chickpeas + feta cheese + grated carrot
+
Add a splash of something acidic, if needed
lemon juice, lime juice, or a favorite vinegar

3 FIX A KILLER PLATE OF PASTA

Every kids' menu in the country seems to have pasta on it. That's because everyone (or nearly everyone) loves pasta. It's easy to make and can be prepared in so many ways. It's also dirt cheap. In fact, with just a few ingredients and a box of pasta, you can feed a few friends for about what you'd spend on a large coffee drink at Starbucks. This is exactly why it makes sense to learn to cook at least one good pasta that you can pull out when hunger strikes.

To tackle this chapter, start with whatever recipe jumps out at you first. Maybe it's the Genius Spaghetti and Tomato Sauce (page 54) or the Pasta with Butter, Egg, and Cheese (page 57).

Make it.

Then make it again. Once you have it down, move on to another one, such as Pesto Pasta (page 64) or the Noodles with Spicy Peanut Sauce (page 59). You'll quickly get the hang of things. You won't have to set a timer to know when the pasta is done, and you might figure out how to adjust recipes depending on your mood. Add chilies to that tomato sauce, for example, or bacon to the Pasta with Butter, Egg, and Cheese. Eventually you can ditch the recipes altogether and create your own dishes using the foundation of the ones in this chapter. That's when home cooking really gets interesting.

GENIUS SPAGHETTI AND TOMATO SAUCE

MAKES 4 TO 6 SERVINGS

I always thought that a good Italian tomato sauce involved hours at the stove and a long list of ingredients. Then I made this for the first time, a recipe invented by the famous Italian cookbook author Marcella Hazan. It was an eye-opener because the sauce was so surprisingly simple yet flavorful. You don't even have to bother chopping the onion; just cut it in half and throw it in. Who needs pasta sauce from a jar with a recipe like this?

1 large yellow onion

10 medium fresh basil leaves

One 28-ounce can whole peeled tomatoes

4 tablespoons butter

1 teaspoon kosher salt, plus more for salting the pasta cooking water

12 ounces spaghetti or other pasta shape

⅓ cup grated Parmesan cheese

KEY EQUIPMENT: chef's knife, cutting board, can opener, medium pot, large pot, cheese grater, colander

PRO TIP: Make a double batch of tomato sauce and store the extra in a freezer bag or covered container in the freezer.

Put the onion on a cutting board and trim off the hairy-looking stem end. Cut the onion in half and remove the peel (no need to chop). Chop the basil.

Empty the can of tomatoes with the juices into a medium pot. Use your hands to squeeze the tomatoes so they break up into smaller pieces. Add the onion halves, butter, and 1 teaspoon salt. Put the pot on the stove over medium-high heat. When the liquid begins to simmer (gently bubble), set a timer for 40 minutes. Adjust the heat as needed to keep the sauce at a simmer, but not boiling

When the sauce is almost done, cook the pasta. Fill a large pot with water and add enough salt that it tastes slightly salty. Put it on the stove over high heat. When the water boils, add the spaghetti, stir, and cook according to package directions until al dente (see page 56). Set a colander in the sink and pour in pasta to drain.

PREP

When the timer for the sauce rings, remove it from heat and use a spoon to scoop out the onion halves and discard. Stir in the basil. Taste the sauce and add more salt, if needed.

Divide the pasta into bowls and spoon some of the sauce over the top. Pass grated Parmesan at the table to sprinkle over the top.

SERVE WITH: Green Salad with Shake-It-Up Dressing on page 86. You can also make a double batch to serve with Homemade Saucy Meatballs on page 152.

What Is Al Dente, Anyway?

Al dente is an Italian phrase that means "to the tooth" and refers to the ideal consistency for cooked pasta. I'm sure some pasta pros can tell when pasta is done just by looking at it, but I need to taste it every time. I use a pair of tongs to snatch a strand of spaghetti or spiral of rotini from the boiling water. Let it cool just enough so that it doesn't burn your mouth and take a bite. You're looking for that sweet spot between hard and crunchy and soft and mushy. Firm but tender is what you're aiming for.

PASTA WITH BUTTER, EGG, AND CHEESE

MAKES 4 TO 6 SERVINGS

My Italian aunt Thereza made this pasta all the time when my cousins and I were little. It was always met with great enthusiasm. Once you get the pasta cooked, it takes about 1 minute to pull it all together. And since it's done in the same pot where you cook the pasta, there's minimal cleanup.

1 teaspoon kosher salt, plus more for the pasta cooking water

1 pound spaghetti or other favorite pasta shape

¾ cup milk, plus more if needed

1 egg

2 tablespoons butter

⅔ cup finely grated Pecorino Romano cheese, plus more to pass at the table (Parmesan can be substituted)

⅛ teaspoon black pepper

KEY EQUIPMENT: large pot, medium bowl, whisk, colander, cheese grater, wooden spoon

PRO TIP: Toss 2 to 3 slices of crumbled cooked bacon or pancetta into the pasta just before serving.

Fill a large pot with water and add enough salt so that the water tastes slightly salty. Put the pot on the stove over high heat. When the water boils, add the spaghetti, stir, and cook according to package directions until al dente (see page 56).

While the spaghetti cooks, put the milk and egg in a medium bowl and whisk together until blended.

Once the pasta is done, place a colander in the sink, and pour in the spaghetti to drain. Immediately return hot pasta to the cooking pot and turn the stove to low heat. Add the milk-egg mixture and butter, and stir just until the milk thickens and coats the noodles, 1 to 2 minutes.

Remove from heat. Add the cheese, 1 teaspoon salt, and pepper, and stir again. If the sauce looks too sticky or dry, add more milk, 1 tablespoon at a time, until the sauce lightly coats the pasta.

Serve immediately with extra grated Pecorino Romano to add at the table.

SERVE WITH: Roasted Broccoli with Lemon and Parmesan on page 104 or the Arugula Salad with Balsamic Vinaigrette on page 91.

Match Sauce to Shape

While there are no hard-and-fast rules for selecting which pasta to use with which sauce, a few basic guidelines may help you choose the best match:

- Pair short shapes, such as penne or rigatoni, with chunkier sauces.
- Serve long, very slender noodles, such as angel hair, with thinner sauces, such as marinara or olive oil–based sauces.
- Sturdier long pastas, such as bucatini or fettuccine, can stand up to thicker cream sauces and heartier meat sauces.

That said, feel free to do what works for you. Like so many standards of cooking, rules are meant to be broken.

NOODLES WITH SPICY PEANUT SAUCE

If you've ever had spicy peanut sauce at a Thai restaurant, you'll recognize the flavors in this dish, which are peanutty, a little salty, and just spicy enough. It's super-easy to make because the sauce is just peanut butter with a few other ingredients whisked in a bowl, then tossed with cooked pasta. For vegetables, use whatever you like in any combination. (I'm partial to snap peas, red bell pepper, and cucumber.)

Kosher salt for the pasta cooking water

1 pound spaghetti

1 lime

½ cup unsweetened, creamy peanut butter

1 tablespoon soy sauce

2 tablespoons seasoned rice vinegar

⅓ cup water

1½ teaspoons sriracha (more if you want it spicier)

3 green onions

2½ cups diced crunchy raw vegetables in any combination, such as cucumbers, bell peppers, celery, carrots, and snap peas

KEY EQUIPMENT: large pot, large bowl, whisk, chef's knife, cutting board, colander

Fill a large pot with water and add enough salt so that the water tastes slightly salty. Put the pot on the stove over high heat. When the water boils, add the spaghetti, stir, and cook according to package directions until al dente (see page 56).

While the pasta cooks, cut the lime in half and squeeze enough juice to fill 1 tablespoon. Put the lime juice into a large bowl with the peanut butter, soy sauce, rice vinegar, water, and sriracha. Stir with a whisk until creamy and smooth. Set aside.

Lay the green onions on a cutting board. Trim off the hairy-looking tips and the dark green ends and discard. Cut the white and light green parts into very thin, round slices.

Once the pasta is done, set a colander in the sink, and pour in the pasta to drain well.

Add the pasta, vegetables, and green onions to the peanut sauce and mix well. If the sauce thickens and the pasta gets sticky as it sits, add another 1 to 2 tablespoons of water (or a splash of sesame oil if you have it) to thin the sauce. Serve immediately.

Avoid the Burn

Maneuvering around the stove with a pot of pasta in boiling water takes extra care. Here are a few tips to prevent kitchen mishaps:

1. Set your colander in the sink before you carry the pasta pot over to drain.
2. Use 2 good pot holders and never pick up a pot with a cloth that is damp.
3. Before you carry a heavy pot over to the stove, do a trial run by lifting the pot up just a little to make sure you can handle the weight. If it's too heavy, ask for help or use a slotted spoon to transfer the pasta from the pot to a bowl and then drain in the sink.
4. Carefully lift the pot and carry it to the sink. Tip it away from you, pouring hot water and pasta into the colander.

SUMMER PASTA BOWL

I've been making this pasta every summer for as long as I can remember. It's a recipe I pull out in June when the tomatoes start to get really good, and I put it away in September once the summer corn has come and gone. It's quick to make, since the vegetables spend just a few minutes on the stove and then get tossed with olive oil, basil, and a shower of Parmesan cheese.

1 teaspoon kosher salt, plus more for the pasta cooking water

3 large cloves garlic

3 ears of corn

3 large ripe tomatoes

1 bunch fresh basil

1 pound penne pasta

¼ cup extra-virgin olive oil

½ lemon

½ teaspoon black pepper

¼ cup Parmesan cheese, plus more to pass at the table

KEY EQUIPMENT: large pot, cutting board, chef's knife, serrated-edge knife, large skillet, colander, cheese grater

Fill a large pot with water and add enough salt so that the water tastes slightly salty. Set on the stove over high heat and bring to a boil.

While the water is heating, prepare the vegetables. Peel the garlic and cut into paper-thin slices. Pull the papery husks off the corn and pull off all the silky threads. Lay the corn cobs on a cutting board and use a chef's knife or serrated-edge knife to cut the kernels off the cobs, working your way around each ear until they're stripped of corn. Cut out the little bit of core at the top of the tomatoes and discard. Cut the tomatoes into thick slices using a serrated-edge knife. Stack the sliced tomatoes upright and slice through them in both directions so you have a roughly chopped pile of tomatoes. Roughly chop enough basil to fill a ½ cup.

When the pasta water boils, add the penne and cook according to package directions until al dente (see page 56).

While the pasta cooks, heat the oil in a large skillet on the stove over medium heat. Add the garlic and sauté for 1 minute or so, stirring regularly and being sure it doesn't burn. Add the corn and sauté until it is just barely tender and no longer tastes raw, about 3 to 4 minutes. Remove the pan from heat and add the tomatoes and basil.

When the pasta is done, put a colander in the sink and pour in the pasta to drain well. Then put the hot pasta back into the pot. Add the corn-tomato-basil mixture. Squeeze the juice of the half lemon over everything. Stir well and add the salt, pepper, and Parmesan cheese. Stir again. Taste and add more salt if needed.

Serve in bowls with extra Parmesan cheese on the side.

SERVE WITH: Butter Lettuce Salad with Green Goodness Dressing on page 93.

PESTO PASTA

Pesto is as simple to make as it is delicious to eat. All you have to do is run your ingredients through a blender and toss the finished pesto with pasta. The heat of the pasta brings the garlic and fresh herbs to life.

1 large bunch fresh basil

1 large bunch fresh mint

1 small clove garlic

¼ cup walnuts

⅓ cup extra-virgin olive oil

2 teaspoons lemon juice

½ teaspoon kosher salt, plus more for the pasta cooking water

¼ cup finely grated Parmesan cheese, plus more to pass at the table

1 pound penne, farfalle, fusilli, or other favorite pasta shape

KEY EQUIPMENT: cutting board, chef's knife, blender, rubber spatula, large bowl, cheese grater, large pot, colander

PRO TIP: Pasta isn't the only way to use pesto. Spread it on pizza dough instead of tomato sauce, toss it with cooked vegetables, or use it for the Pesto Quinoa on page 49.

Pull the leaves from the stems of the basil until you fill 1½ cups, packing it down a bit with your hand. Repeat with the mint leaves, filling a 1-cup measure. Peel the garlic.

Put the basil, mint, garlic, walnuts, olive oil, lemon juice, and salt in a blender and run until blended into a smooth green paste, stopping to scrape down the sides with the rubber spatula and run again, as needed. Add the Parmesan and run the blender again until mixed in. Use the rubber spatula to scrape pesto into a large bowl. All the blending should take less than a minute.

Fill a large pot with water and add enough salt so that the water tastes slightly salty. Set it over high heat and bring to a boil. Cook the pasta according to package directions until al dente (see page 56).

Set a colander in the sink and pour in the pasta to drain well. Add the hot pasta to the pesto and stir until the pesto evenly coats the pasta.

Serve with extra grated Parmesan on the side.

SERVE WITH: Buttery Green Beans on page 102.

A Primer on Pasta

Back in the day, the supermarket offered few choices when it came to pasta. But if you've shopped for pasta any time recently, you know that today's options are endless (and maybe a little confusing). Here's what you need to know to navigate the pasta aisle:

Dried. All the recipes in this book call for dried pasta, the variety found on store shelves near the canned tomatoes and other dry goods. Dried pasta is very inexpensive and shelf stable, which means it will last a good long while.

Fresh. Fresh pasta is available in the refrigerated section of the market. Unlike dried pasta, it contains egg and cooks in about half the time (or less). When using fresh pasta in a recipe, you'll need about 50 percent more by weight than if using dried. So if a recipe calls for 1 pound of pasta, use 1½ pounds of fresh pasta.

Gluten-free. Traditionally pasta is made with semolina, a type of wheat flour that's fine for most people but not for anyone with an allergy or intolerance to wheat or gluten. Luckily most markets sell wheat- and gluten-free alternatives, including brown rice pasta, chickpea pasta, and quinoa pasta, just to name a few. Gluten-free pasta can be sticky once cooked, so be sure to give it a generous rinse at the tap to minimize stickiness.

Whole wheat/multigrain. The upside of whole wheat and many multigrain pastas is that they haven't been stripped of the bran and germ in the grains from which they're made. Translation: they have more vitamins, minerals, and fiber. If you've never had whole grain pasta before, give it a try. It may take time to develop a taste for it, but eventually you just might take to it.

Vegetable-infused. Some pastas, both fresh and dried, are infused with vegetables, such as spinach or bell pepper. The vegetables add color but don't typically have a big impact on flavor or nutritional value.

Choose Your Own Adventure:
DIY PASTA BOWLS

Invent your own homespun pasta by mixing and matching among various shapes, sauces, and fixings. Adding grated cheese at the end is almost always a good idea.

Pick a pasta
spaghetti, rotini, fusilli, fettuccini, penne, rigatoni, farfalle, bucatini

Add a sauce
- Genius Tomato Sauce (page 54)
- Butter, Egg, and Cheese (page 57)
- Pesto (page 64)

Top with any goodies, such as
- arugula
- cooked asparagus
- cooked bacon
- sautéed bell peppers
- cooked broccoli
- cherry tomatoes
- cooked chicken
- chili flakes
- cooked ground beef
- cooked Italian sausage
- lemon zest
- sautéed mushrooms
- sliced olives
- cooked pancetta
- cooked peas

Finish with cheese
- Parmesan cheese
- Pecorino Romano

4 TURN A POT OF BEANS INTO A MEAL

Learning to cook beans is one of the smartest moves for a new cook. Beans are dirt cheap, good for you, and super-versatile; they're suitable for everything from soups to salads, and countless side dishes. Before I dig in here, let me clarify that I'm not referring to the fresh, bright green beans that you find in the produce section of the market. I'm talking about dried beans—pinto, navy, kidney, and black beans, for example—that come in a rainbow of colors and a variety of sizes. You can buy them in the bulk bin or dry goods section of the store or already cooked and packed in cans. And even though it's unlikely that beans come to mind when you think of favorite foods, consider how many favorite foods are made with beans:

Tacos	Gumbo	Minestrone
Chili	Enchiladas	Nachos

In this chapter you'll start off by learning to cook a basic pot of black beans. From there, use the beans to prepare the other recipes in the chapter. Of course, you can always use canned beans if you don't have the time or interest to make your own.

SIMPLE BLACK BEANS

Everyone has a different opinion about the best way to cook dried beans. Some insist that you soak them overnight before cooking, others claim that's a waste of time, and nobody can agree about when to add salt to the pot. I've ignored all that chatter and just do beans the way my friend Sara does them. She's from Guatemala, where beans are eaten on a daily basis, and she manages to make a perfect pot every time.

1 pound dried black beans (about 2 cups)

2 large cloves garlic

½ yellow onion

8 cups water

2 teaspoons kosher salt

KEY EQUIPMENT: colander, medium saucepan

PRO TIP: You can use this same technique for lots of other types of beans. Typically the bigger the bean, the more water you'll need and the longer it will take to cook.

Pour the beans into a colander. Run your hands through them, looking for any tiny stones or other debris to throw out. Rinse the beans under water and let drain.

Peel the garlic and onion. Put the garlic, onion, beans, and water into a medium saucepan. Put the pan on the stove over high heat and bring to a boil. Once the water reaches a full boil, reduce the heat just a touch so that it continues to boil, just not super vigorously. Boil the beans, checking them occasionally to make sure there is plenty of water in the pot. If you begin to see beans close to the surface, add another cup or so of very hot tap water, and turn the heat up to high for a few minutes until the water boils again.

After 30 minutes, add the salt, stir, and taste a couple of beans. You want them just tender, but not mushy. The length of cooking time can vary significantly, from 30 minutes to 1 hour or more. Check the beans from time to time until they're done. Remove the pot from the heat. Leave the beans in their cooking liquid, scooping them up with a slotted spoon as needed to serve or use in another recipe.

Store the beans in their cooking liquid in a covered container in the fridge, where they will keep for up to 5 days.

SERVE WITH: Easy Brown Rice on page 45. Top with a squeeze of lime juice and a little chopped cilantro.

What to Do with All Those Beans?

If you're going to the trouble of cooking beans from scratch, make it worth your while and do up a big batch. Then keep half in a container in the fridge and store the rest in a resealable bag in the freezer. (Be sure to store beans in their cooking liquid; don't drain.) Beans freeze well for several months. To defrost, put the bag on the counter for an hour, empty them into a saucepan, and warm on the stove.

Did You Know?

Dried black beans triple in volume as they cook. One cup swells to 3 cups.

SMASHED BEAN AND CHEESE TOSTADAS

MAKES 2 TOSTADAS

If you're a taco fan, this recipe should be right up your alley, since a tostada is basically just an open-faced taco. The key to success is to get the bottom of the tortilla super-crisp before piling on the toppings. You don't have to worry about it being pretty because everything gets mashed together into a delicious, finger-licking mess.

Two 6-inch corn tortillas

½ cup cooked black or pinto beans, drained

1 tablespoon Mexican salsa

½ cup grated sharp Cheddar cheese

2 teaspoons canola or other vegetable oil

½ large avocado

Pinch salt

½ lime

KEY EQUIPMENT: cheese grater, large skillet, spatula, cutting board, chef's knife

PRO TIP: You can really play around with what goes on these tostadas. Fry an egg, shred leftover chicken or beef, or sauté some greens to top them off.

Lay the tortillas on the counter. Divide the beans and salsa between the 2 tortillas. Use a fork to mash everything together. Spread the smashed beans over the surface of the tortillas. Sprinkle the cheese on top.

Put a skillet (large enough to fit both tortillas) on the stove over high heat. Add the oil, swirling it around so it coats the pan. When the pan is good and hot, set the tortillas in the oil. Cook until the bottoms are lightly browned and crisp and the cheese is mostly melted, 2 to 3 minutes.

Use a spatula to transfer the tortillas to a cutting board. Scoop the avocado out of its skin. Put it on a cutting board and cut into small cubes. Scatter the avocado over the tostadas. Add a pinch of salt and a squeeze of lime juice over everything.

Use a chef's knife to cut each tortilla into quarters. Dig in.

SERVE WITH: Cucumber or jicama slices doused with lime juice and sprinkled with chili powder or Tajin (a Mexican spice blend).

Canned Beans: Let It Drain

There's no shame in buying canned beans instead of cooking them yourself. I do it all the time. *But* you might find that the liquid in the cans is sort of gunky and unappealing. Here are two ways to drain the beans before using:

1. With a colander: Open the can and dump everything into a colander. Rinse under cold water. Drain well.

2. Without a colander: Leave the top of the can in place after you've opened it. With your fingers pressing on the top, invert the can and drain the liquid into the sink. Return it upright, remove the lid (careful not to cut yourself on the edge), fill the can with water, return the top of the can, invert it, and drain again.

BREAKFAST BURRITOS

Even though these are called breakfast burritos and are full of ingredients usually found at the breakfast table, you can eat them any time of day. The recipe makes 2 but can easily be doubled or tripled to feed a bigger crowd. If you care to add cheese, just top the tortillas with a little grated Cheddar or Monterey Jack before you warm them in the microwave.

½ avocado

2 eggs

¼ teaspoon kosher salt

2 slices bacon

2 large flour tortillas

¼ cup cooked black beans or pinto beans, drained

3 tablespoons pico de gallo or salsa fresca

KEY EQUIPMENT: chef's knife, cutting board, small bowl, medium skillet, paper towels, microwave

Scoop the avocado out of its skin and put it on a cutting board. Use a chef's knife to cut the avocado into thin slices. Set aside.

Crack the eggs into a small bowl, add the salt, and use a fork to whisk until blended and an even color.

Heat a medium skillet on the stove over medium heat. Lay the bacon slices in the pan and cook on one side until nicely browned, about 4 minutes. Use a fork to turn the bacon over and cook the other side until brown, about 3 to 4 minutes. Take care so the grease doesn't splatter and burn your hand. Remove cooked bacon from pan and place on a stack of paper towels to absorb the grease. When the bacon is cool enough to touch, break each slice into 5 or 6 pieces.

With great care, use a pot holder to lift the pan and drain the grease. (I usually drain it into an empty can set in the sink, since grease isn't good for plumbing.) Return the pan to the stove and use a couple of paper towels to wipe out any bits of bacon (you want the pan lightly

coated with grease, just not bacon pieces). Turn the heat to medium. When it's hot, pour in the eggs. Scramble until just cooked through (see page 26 for instructions, if needed). Remove from heat.

Heat the tortillas in the microwave on high for 30 seconds and lay them side by side on the kitchen counter. Divide the eggs, avocado, beans, bacon, and salsa between the 2 tortillas, lining everything up in the center with about an inch of space at the top and bottom. Fold in the sides of 1 tortilla as you roll it up tight, so the ingredients are tucked inside. Repeat with the remaining tortilla.

7 Good Things to Do with a Cup of Beans

Stir into soup. Stir favorite beans into brothy soups, such as minestrone or chicken and vegetable.

Make a salad. Most varieties of beans are tasty mixed with a basic vinaigrette and diced vegetables. Serve warm or at room temperature.

Smash onto toast. Use the back of a fork to smash warm beans onto toast made from crusty bread. Drizzle with olive oil and lemon juice and season with salt and pepper.

Toss with tuna. Make tuna salad a little less ordinary by adding white beans or chickpeas (which aren't technically beans, but close enough) along with a generous squeeze of lemon.

Do a dip. Black beans make a tasty dip for tortilla chips, and nearly any type of bean can be blended into something similar to hummus.

Add to pasta. Stir beans into tomato-based, vegetable-heavy, or meaty pasta dishes. Finish with plenty of Parmesan.

Go with grains. Beans and grains go together—rice and red beans, barley and navy beans, and quinoa and adzuki beans, just to name a few.

CREAMY BLACK BEAN SOUP

Chipotle peppers en adobo are the secret to this soup. They're ordinary jalapeño peppers that have been smoked, smothered in a tangy sauce, and packed in small cans (you can find them in the supermarket, near the Mexican salsa). Just half of a pepper is all it takes to give the soup loads of flavor without being too spicy. Top with a spoonful of sour cream and you'll find it's hard to eat just one bowl.

1 medium yellow onion

2 cloves garlic

1 chipotle pepper en adobo (sold in small cans)

1 tablespoon extra-virgin olive oil

1 teaspoon oregano

¼ teaspoon ground cumin

1 teaspoon kosher salt

3 cups black beans, drained (if using canned beans, you'll need two 15½-ounce cans)

1¼ cups low-sodium vegetable broth or chicken broth

½ large lemon

¼ cup sour cream, for garnish

KEY EQUIPMENT: cutting board, chef's knife, medium skillet, ladle, food processor or blender

Peel and finely chop the onion. Peel and thinly sliced the garlic. Put the chipotle pepper on a cutting board and cut it in half. Use a chef's knife to chop half of the pepper until it turns into a smooth paste. Save the other half for another use.

Heat the olive oil in a medium skillet on the stove over medium heat. Add the onion and sauté, stirring regularly until tender, 5 minutes. Add the garlic and continue to sauté for 1 minute. Add the chipotle pepper, oregano, cumin, salt, beans, and broth. Turn the heat to high until broth boils, then drop the heat to about medium until the soup simmers. Simmer 5 minutes.

Scoop 1 cup of the soup from the pot and place it in a blender or food processor. Blend until smooth, then add it back to the soup pot. Squeeze enough lemon juice to measure 1 tablespoon and add it to the soup. Stir well. Add a little more broth or water if soup is too thick.

Serve in bowls topped with a spoonful of sour cream.

A Rainbow of Beans

It's easy to stick with what's familiar, but with so many different beans to try, it's worth experimenting. Here are 12 common varieties of beans to look for and cook with:

Adzuki. Small, reddish brown
Black. Small, oval, black skin
Blackeye. White skin with tiny black "eye"
Cannellini. Large, white
Cranberry. Smallish, white with red markings that diminish when cooked
Great Northern. Medium, white, flat
Kidney. Large, kidney shaped, reddish brown
Lima. Large, flat, ivory
Navy. Smallish, white
Pink. Small, pale pink that darkens as it cooks
Pinto. Medium, speckled beige and reddish-brown that turns solid once cooked
Red. Dark red, like a kidney bean only small

Did You Know?

Apparently the US government likes their beans. A dish called Senate Bean Soup has been on the menu in the US Senate dining room every day for more than 100 years.

LOADED NACHOS

If your only experience with nachos is the kind with bright yellow cheese that comes from a pump, you're in for a treat. Homemade nachos are easy to make and crazy good to eat. These are loaded with cheese, beans, sour cream, and salsa. Pickled jalapeños are the crowning touch; they really take nachos to the next level. They're sold in cans or jars in the Mexican food section of the market. If you don't like things too spicy, look for "mild" or "tamed" on the label.

5 big handfuls tortilla chips (about 8 ounces)

3 cups grated sharp Cheddar cheese

1 cup cooked black beans or pinto beans, drained

3 tablespoons sour cream

⅓ cup Mexican salsa

½ cup pickled jalapeños

KEY EQUIPMENT: cheese grater, large baking sheet, aluminum foil

PRO TIP: Substitute the Spicy Sweet Potato Rounds (page 107) for the tortilla chips in this recipe. It's a tasty and good-for-you twist on traditional nachos.

Preheat oven to 425°F.

Cover a large baking sheet with aluminum foil (for easy cleanup). Spread the tortilla chips across the baking sheet, overlapping slightly. Sprinkle the cheese over the chips followed by the black beans. Bake until the cheese melts and bubbles, about 5 minutes.

Remove from oven and spoon small dollops of sour cream and salsa over the nachos. Scatter the jalapeños over everything. Serve immediately.

Choose Your Own Adventure:
BLACK BEAN SOUP OR CHILI BAR

Turn an ordinary bowl of black bean soup or chili into a creative way to feed a crowd of friends. Pull out all your favorite fixings and let everyone top their bowls just the way they like.

Creamy Black Bean Soup (page 78) or Big Pot of Turkey Chili (page 157)

Hot stuff
pickled jalapeños
Mexican salsa
hot pepper sauce

Flavor
chopped red onions
sliced green onions
lime wedges
fresh cilantro

Crunch
tortilla chips
pepitas
oyster crackers
crumbled bacon

Creamy/Cheesy
grated Monterey Jack cheese
grated Cheddar cheese
sour cream
diced avocado
crumbled cotija cheese

5 BUILD A BETTER SALAD

If you take ice cream and pizza out of the running, salad is probably my favorite food. It's a broad category that covers everything from iceberg lettuce tossed with Italian dressing to colorful salads of vegetables, beans, grains, fish, chicken, and practically anything else you can think of (there's even Cookie Salad, popular in the Midwest and made with cookies and Cool Whip).

Making a really good salad—one you crave and want to eat on repeat—is not particularly challenging. But it does involve a few key factors:

Homemade dressing. Yes, you can find decent (and sometimes even good) bottled dressing at the supermarket, but I have never found a store-bought dressing as good as one I can make myself. And since making your own is easy, why not?

Good greens. Even a delicious dressing can't mask crummy lettuce. Look for greens with perky leaves, not ones that are wilted or bruised. If lettuce looks tired, as though it's spent a little too long on the shelf, leave it at the market.

Creativity. Salads are tailor-made for tinkering. Yes, you can start with a basic salad recipe, but then add ingredients depending on what you like and what's in the fridge. Use different vegetables, swap in fruit, add herbs, include nuts or cheese, or turn a side salad into a main dish by adding chicken, shrimp, lentils, or chickpeas. The sky's the limit.

GREEN SALAD WITH SHAKE-IT-UP DRESSING

This is a starter salad. It's a popular one in my house because you can include whatever vegetables you like and leave out the ones you don't. Everyone loves the homemade croutons, so I often make twice as many as I need; the extras get demolished by the time dinner is ready.

1 loaf crusty bread, such as a baguette, bâtard, or Italian bread

1 tablespoon plus ⅓ cup extra-virgin olive oil, divided

¼ teaspoon kosher salt, divided

2 tablespoons red wine vinegar

1 teaspoon Dijon mustard

½ teaspoon honey

Freshly ground black pepper

1 head red leaf or butter lettuce (also called Bibb)

1½ cups favorite cut-up salad vegetables, such as cucumbers, carrots, cherry tomatoes, avocado, celery, radishes, and/or jicama (choose as many as you like)

KEY EQUIPMENT: cutting board, serrated-edge knife, baking sheet, chef's knife, small glass jar with a lid, salad spinner or colander, large bowl, salad servers

Preheat oven or toaster oven to 400°F.

Use a serrated-edge knife to cut the bread into 1-inch cubes. Cut enough bread to fill 2 cups and pile onto a baking sheet (save leftover bread for another use). Drizzle bread cubes with 1 tablespoon olive oil and use your hands to toss until coated. Sprinkle ⅛ teaspoon salt over the top and toss again.

Bake until just beginning to brown lightly, about 5 minutes. Remove from the oven and leave on the counter to cool.

Put the vinegar, mustard, honey, remaining ⅛ teaspoon salt, a few grinds of black pepper, and the remaining ⅓ cup oil into a small jar. Screw on the lid and shake vigorously for about 10 seconds until the ingredients are smooth and blended. Dip a lettuce leaf into the dressing to be sure the taste is to your liking. Add more salt, pepper, oil, or vinegar, if needed.

Wash and dry the lettuce (see page 88). Tear the larger leaves into a few pieces. Put the lettuce into a large bowl. Add the vegetables. Drizzle a few tablespoons of dressing over the salad. Use salad servers to toss well. Taste. Add the croutons and a little more dressing if needed

PRO TIP: Play around with this dressing to make it your own. Try using a different type of vinegar, add a teaspoon of minced garlic or shallot, or whisk in finely chopped fresh basil, tarragon, or other herbs.

and toss again. Taste. Add a pinch of salt and freshly ground black pepper, if desired.

Serve immediately. Save any leftover dressing in the fridge for another use.

How to Wash Lettuce

Before you make a salad, you've got to wash the lettuce. Be gentle, since lettuce is delicate. And dry it well. Nobody likes soggy salad; plus, dressings won't stick to damp lettuce. Here's how: Gently pull the leaves off the core of the lettuce and plunge them into a big bowl of cold water. Swish the water around to clean the leaves. Rub off any obvious dirt with your thumbs. The dirt will drift to the bottom of the bowl. Lift the lettuce from the water into a large colander and run under cold water to remove any remaining dirt. Shake the colander well and either dry the leaves gently on paper towels or transfer to a salad spinner and crank the spinner until the lettuce is very dry.

Did You Know?

Dijon mustard originated in the town of Dijon, France, which is probably why many consider it the mustard capital of the world.

CHOPPED GREEK SALAD

Everyone loves a chopped salad, and this one is no exception. It's crunchy and lemony, full of popular salad fixings, and finished with good, salty feta cheese. The pita chips are my favorite part because they act like croutons and make the salad super addictive.

1 small clove garlic

2 lemons

⅓ cup extra-virgin olive oil

¼ teaspoon ground cumin

¼ teaspoon kosher salt

⅛ teaspoon black pepper

1 head romaine lettuce

1 cup cherry tomatoes

1 English cucumber

20 pita chips

½ cup crumbled feta cheese

KEY EQUIPMENT: cutting board, chef's knife, serrated-edge knife, small bowl, salad spinner or colander, large bowl, salad servers

PRO TIP: Add 1 cup chickpeas (drained from a can) to make this a more filling salad.

Peel and mince the garlic and put into a small bowl. Cut the lemons in half and squeeze enough juice that you have 3 tablespoons (you may not need both lemons), add to the garlic along with the olive oil, cumin, salt, and pepper. Use a fork to whisk the ingredients together until smooth.

Wash and dry the lettuce (see page 88). Stack the leaves on a cutting board and cut across into 1-inch-wide strips. Put 6 cups of the crunchier, paler green lettuce into a large bowl. Save any remaining lettuce for another use. Cut the cherry tomatoes in half (a serrated-edge knife may be useful here) and add to the bowl. Cut half the cucumber into thin slices and add to the bowl. Save the remaining cucumber or another use.

Drizzle most of the dressing over the salad and use salad servers to toss it together. If the salad needs more dressing, add enough so it's lightly coated and tastes good. Break the pita chips into a few pieces and add to the salad along with the feta. Toss well and serve.

How to Dress a Salad

To *dress a salad* means to toss the greens and vegetables with the dressing. Here's roughly how it goes:

1. Be sure your lettuce is washed and very dry before you begin. (See page 88.)
2. Put the lettuce into a bowl that has some extra room so you can toss the salad without it spilling over the side.
3. Drizzle on some dressing. Use less than you think you need. (If it requires more, you can always add it, but once it's on, there's no going back.)
4. Use salad servers, tongs, or clean hands to toss the salad in the bowl until evenly dressed. Taste a leaf. Each one should be very lightly coated in dressing, not wet or soggy. If it seems like it needs more, drizzle on a little and toss again. Do this until you have it right.

ARUGULA SALAD WITH BALSAMIC VINAIGRETTE

MAKES 4 SERVINGS

Vinaigrette is really just a fancy sounding word for a salad dressing made with oil and vinegar. This particular one is my all-time favorite, good on nearly any kind of lettuce. I especially like it on arugula because the vinegar is sweet and the greens are peppery. Together they make a nice balance. You'll have leftover dressing, so save it to drizzle over cooked vegetables, such as green beans or potatoes.

1 small shallot

1 tablespoon plus 1 teaspoon balsamic vinegar

2 teaspoons red wine vinegar

¾ teaspoon soy sauce

1½ teaspoons whole grain Dijon mustard (sold in jars near the regular Dijon)

⅓ cup extra-virgin olive oil

6 packed cups baby arugula (6 big handfuls)

1 small chunk Parmesan cheese (the size of a deck of cards is more than enough)

KEY EQUIPMENT: cutting board, chef's knife, small bowl, salad spinner or colander, large bowl, salad servers, vegetable peeler

PRO TIP: Add one of the following: ½ cup sliced strawberries, 2 seedless tangerines, 1 cubed avocado, or 1 small, sliced apple.

Peel and dice enough shallot to fill 2 teaspoons (use the same method as chopping onions, page 12). Put the diced shallot in a small bowl with the balsamic vinegar, red wine vinegar, soy sauce, and mustard. Whisk with a fork until blended.

Use one hand to slowly drizzle the olive oil into the bowl while simultaneously whisking the dressing with your other hand. Continue to whisk until all of the ingredients are blended with no separation of oil from vinegar.

Wash and dry the arugula, page 88 (no need if using prewashed arugula). Put the arugula into a large bowl. Drizzle about half of the dressing over the greens and use salad servers to turn the greens in the dressing until evenly coated. Drizzle on a little more dressing, if needed.

Hold the chunk of Parmesan in one hand over the bowl. In the other hand, hold a vegetable peeler and run it across the surface of the cheese to peel about 20 thin shavings into the salad. Add more if you love Parmesan. Toss the salad again and serve. Store extra dressing in the fridge for up to 1 week.

3 Quick and Easy Salads

A salad doesn't have to involve precise measurements or lots of ingredients to be good. Here are a few simple ones that I make all the time:

Japanese Cucumber Salad

Cut an English cucumber or several Persian cucumbers into thin slices. Put into a bowl and douse with a few tablespoons of seasoned rice vinegar and a pinch of salt. Sprinkle sesame seeds over the top.

PRO TIP: This is a good one to serve on the side when you order take-out sushi.

Caprese Salad

Cut ripe tomatoes into ¼-inch-thick slices. Cut half as many slices of fresh mozzarella. Layer them on a plate and drizzle lightly with olive oil. Sprinkle on salt, pepper, and a shower of roughly chopped fresh basil.

PRO TIP: Make this in summer when the tomatoes are good.

Crunchy Winter Salad

In a shallow bowl, toss together equal amounts of paper-thin slices of carrot, fennel, and apple. Dress lightly with lemon juice, olive oil, salt, and pepper. Scatter sliced almonds over the top.

PRO TIP: Add shaved Parmesan cheese if you have some in the fridge.

Did You Know?

Contrary to popular belief, Caesar salad wasn't invented by Julius Caesar. It was created by Caesar Cardini, who owned a restaurant in Tijuana, Mexico.

BUTTER LETTUCE WITH GREEN GOODNESS DRESSING

MAKES 4 TO 5 SERVINGS

The dressing in this salad is based on an old recipe called Green Goddess from a famous hotel in San Francisco. I've turned it into Green Goodness by adding avocado, which makes it extra green, extra creamy, and extra good for you. It reminds me of ranch dip, which means any leftover dressing is a great dip for raw crunchy vegetables.

3 green onions

15 medium fresh basil leaves

½ medium ripe avocado

1 lemon

½ cup sour cream

¼ cup mayonnaise

1 tablespoon extra-virgin olive oil

½ teaspoon kosher salt

¼ teaspoon black pepper

1 head butter lettuce (also called Bibb lettuce)

1 large ripe tomato

KEY EQUIPMENT: cutting board, chef's knife, serrated-edge knife, blender or food processor, rubber spatula, salad spinner or colander, large bowl, salad servers

Lay the green onions on a cutting board. Trim off the hairy-looking tips and the dark green ends and discard. Cut the remaining white and light green parts into 3 or 4 pieces. Roughly chop the basil.

Scoop out the flesh of the avocado and put into a food processor or blender. Cut the lemon in half and squeeze enough juice to fill 2 tablespoons. Add the juice to the food processor along with the green onions, basil, sour cream, mayonnaise, olive oil, salt, and pepper. Blend until the dressing is silky smooth, stopping to scrape down the sides as needed.

Wash and dry the lettuce (see page 88). Tear the large leaves into a few pieces. Put all of the lettuce into a large salad bowl.

Use a knife to cut out the stem at the top of the tomato and discard. Cut the tomato in half through the stem and then cut each half into 5 or 6 wedges. Add to the bowl with the lettuce.

Spoon a few tablespoons of dressing over the salad. Toss well. Add a little more dressing if needed and toss again and serve immediately. You will have leftover dressing, which you can save in the fridge for up to 4 days.

What about Prewashed Lettuce?

Most supermarkets sell bags of leafy greens that are already washed, in some cases chopped, and sold in sealed cellophane bags or plastic tubs. Buying prewashed greens will save you time, but they're usually more expensive and not always in great shape. I find the arugula, baby spinach, baby kale, and mixed baby greens to be pretty good, but haven't had much success with packaged lettuce or cabbage. In those cases, I'd suggest you do the work of washing it yourself.

EASY ASIAN-STYLE SLAW

Although this recipe is called a slaw, it bears little resemblance to the mayonnaise-heavy coleslaws you find at summer picnics and cookouts. Instead, it's a light, chopped mix of crunchy vegetables tossed with a dressing that draws from the Asian pantry: sesame oil, rice vinegar, sriracha, and fish sauce. The fish sauce gives the salad a bump of salty, tangy flavor. You can find it, along with the sriracha, in the Asian section of supermarkets.

2 teaspoons toasted sesame oil

3 tablespoons seasoned rice vinegar

1 tablespoon honey

1½ teaspoons Asian fish sauce

¾ teaspoon sriracha

3 green onions

1 medium head green cabbage

Small bunch fresh mint

1 large red or yellow bell pepper

1 large carrot

⅓ cup roasted, salted peanuts

KEY EQUIPMENT: large bowl, cutting board, chef's knife, paring knife, vegetable peeler, cheese grater, salad servers, whisk

Put the sesame oil, rice vinegar, honey, fish sauce, and sriracha into a large bowl. Whisk briskly until blended. Set aside.

Lay the green onions on a cutting board. Trim off the hairy-looking tips and the dark green ends and discard. Cut the remaining white and light green parts into very thin slices.

Put the cabbage on a cutting board and cut it in half through the core. Wrap one half in plastic and store in the fridge for another use. Cut the remaining half in half again, slicing through the core. Use a chef's knife to trim out the wedge of core in each of the 2 sections and discard. Shred the cabbage as you would for coleslaw, using a chef's knife to cut it into very thin slices (⅛ inch thick or so) across the short edge of the cabbage. You should end up with a pile of thin strips.

Chop enough mint leaves to measure 1 tablespoon. Use a paring knife to cut the bell pepper in half starting at one edge of the stem and working your way around to the other side. Break the halves apart. Pull the stem off the pepper and discard. Firmly tap the halves on the counter to dislodge the seeds. Discard seeds. Cut the pepper into very thin strips and cut

PRO TIP: Unlike typical lettuce salads, this slaw can be dressed in advance. If you have leftover slaw, store it in a covered container in the fridge, since it will be good the next day.

those strips in half. Peel and grate the carrot.

Add the cabbage, green onions, pepper, carrot, and mint to the bowl with the dressing. Use salad servers to thoroughly toss the vegetables with the dressing. Transfer to a serving bowl or platter and sprinkle the peanuts over the top. Serve immediately or cover and store in the fridge until ready to eat.

SERVE WITH: Make this a main dish by adding cooked chicken. Buy a supermarket rotisserie chicken, pull the meat off the bones, cut or shred it, and toss as much as you like with the slaw. If it needs more dressing, drizzle on a little more rice vinegar and sesame oil.

Salad Doesn't Like to Sit

The general rule of thumb is to serve a salad as soon as it's dressed, otherwise it will wilt. The exceptions are salads made with hearty greens, such as cabbage and kale, which are often better after they've marinated in dressing for a while.

Did You Know?

A peanut isn't a nut at all. It's a legume, along with chickpeas, lentils, and soybeans.

Choose Your Own Adventure:
RAINBOW SALADS

Once you know how to wash lettuce and make dressing, there's no reason why you can't create your own colorful salads. A couple of tips: Before you toss everything into a bowl, consider if the flavors and textures go together. Start with a few items, taste, and then build from there. You can always add, but you can't take away. Once your salad is tossed, taste it and add salt, pepper, and a little more dressing, as needed.

Greens
butter, red leaf, romaine, baby greens, arugula, endive, spinach, kale, cabbage

Vegetables
artichoke hearts, bell pepper, carrot, celery, corn, cucumber, fennel, tomato, onion, snap peas, radishes, jicama, mushrooms, broccoli

Fruits
apple, blueberries, grapefruit, mandarins, orange, pear, raspberries, blueberries, pomegranate seeds, grapes, peach, strawberries

Cheese
feta, goat cheese, Parmesan, blue cheese

Little extras
walnuts, almonds, sunflower seeds, pumpkin seeds, chickpeas, edamame, olives, crumbled bacon, chopped herbs, croutons, raisins, chopped dates, dried cranberries

Dressing
- Shake-It-Up Dressing (page 86)
- Balsamic Vinaigrette (page 91)
- Green Goodness Dressing (page 93)
- Asian-Style Slaw Dressing (page 95)
- olive oil and vinegar,
- olive oil and lemon juice

6 COOK VEGETABLES YOU WANT TO EAT

If you're like most people, you've been told to "eat your vegetables" since you were little—as if eating vegetables is a chore, like doing homework or taking out the trash.

It's certainly true that eating vegetables is smart, because they're ridiculously good for you. But they're also just really good. If you learn to cook vegetables well and choose the ones you like, you may start eating them because you want to, not because someone is threatening to withhold dessert if you don't.

The 5 recipes in this chapter are like a starter kit of vegetable cooking. You'll learn a variety of techniques—blanching, roasting, steaming, and sautéing—which you'll be able to apply to lots of other vegetables.

BUTTERY GREEN BEANS

Too often green beans get way overcooked, turning a perfectly appealing veggie into a mushy mess—something no one wants to eat. Preparing them well is actually easy. It involves plunging them into boiling water until they're just right, then tossing them with butter and seasonings.

¼ heaping teaspoon kosher salt, plus more for salting the cooking water

1 pound green beans

5 medium basil leaves

1 tablespoon butter

Freshly ground black pepper

KEY EQUIPMENT: medium saucepan, cutting board, chef's knife, colander, medium bowl

PRO TIP: Summer is the season for green beans and fresh basil, so that's the best time of year to make these buttery beans.

Fill a medium saucepan with water about 2 inches below the top. Add enough salt so that the water tastes slightly salty. Set it on the stove over high heat.

While the water heats up, prep the beans. Use your fingers to snap off the very tip of the stem ends of the green beans (not the smooth, pointy tips) and discard. Chop the basil.

When the water boils, add the beans. Cook until the beans are just barely tender (anywhere from 2 to 5 minutes, depending on their size and freshness). Test for doneness by fishing a bean out of the cooking water with a pair of tongs. Taste it for doneness (careful not to burn your tongue!) and continue to cook, if needed. Keep in mind that the beans will continue to cook after they're drained, so you may want to pull them off the heat and drain just before they seem ready.

Set a colander in the sink. Pour the beans into the colander and drain well. Place drained beans in a medium bowl. Immediately add basil, butter, and salt to the hot beans. The heat of the beans will melt the butter. Toss well. Use a pepper grinder to add several turns of black pepper and toss again.

Taste and add more salt or pepper if needed and serve immediately.

How to Shock a Vegetable

Shocking a vegetable is a real cooking term. It means plunging vegetables that have been boiled into an icy bowl of water to stop the cooking process in its tracks. It helps veggies such as broccoli, green beans, and asparagus maintain their vibrant color and prevents them from overcooking. I usually only shock vegetables if I'm not planning to serve them right away and want them to stay colorful and crisp.

Get to Know What Grows

Even though you can buy a huge variety of fruits and vegetables all year, produce is best when you buy locally and when it's in season. Yes, you can find strawberries in January, but they're so much sweeter in June. Get to know what grows near you during the various seasons and do your best to eat them abundantly when they're around. A local farmers' market or farm stand is a good place to start. Everything tastes better and will likely be cheaper.

Here are some favorites from the four seasons:

Spring. Artichokes, asparagus, English peas, strawberries, rhubarb
Summer. Zucchini, corn, green beans, tomatoes, cherries, berries, apricots, peaches, plums, watermelon
Fall. Pumpkin, butternut squash, apples, pears, figs, grapes, cranberries, pomegranate
Winter. Beets, cabbage, Brussels sprouts, avocado, grapefruit, lemons, oranges, mandarins

ROASTED BROCCOLI WITH LEMON AND PARMESAN

Maybe it's because it looks like little trees or because it's easy to dunk into ketchup, but broccoli seems to be one of the first vegetables we take to as kids. In this recipe, broccoli grows up a bit and, in my opinion, is far tastier than when doused with ketchup. These crispy florets get snatched up often before I can get them to the dinner table.

1½ pounds broccoli

2½ tablespoons extra-virgin olive oil

1 teaspoon kosher salt

¼ teaspoon black pepper

½ lemon

2 heaping tablespoons finely grated Parmesan cheese

Pinch of crushed red pepper flakes (optional)

KEY EQUIPMENT: cutting board, chef's knife, large baking sheet, cheese grater

Preheat oven to 425°F.

Put the broccoli on a cutting board and use a chef's knife to cut the heads off the stems. Cut the broccoli heads into small florets that are about 1½ to 2 inches long and about the same across the top. (What really matters is that the pieces are all roughly the same size.)

Lay the stems on a cutting board and slice off the tough outer skin on all sides. Cut the tender flesh that remains into 2-inch-long pieces.

Pile the broccoli onto a baking sheet. Drizzle the olive oil and sprinkle the salt and pepper over the broccoli. Use your hands to toss everything together and spread it out on the baking sheet.

Put the broccoli in the oven and set a timer for 10 minutes. When the timer rings, pull out the broccoli, give it a good stir, and return it to the oven. Continue to roast the broccoli until tender and lightly browned in places, about 5 to 8 minutes more. Remove from oven.

Squeeze enough lemon juice to measure 1 tablespoon. Push the broccoli together on the baking sheet and drizzle lemon juice over it.

Sprinkle with the Parmesan. Toss well. Add the crushed red pepper, if using.

Serve straight from the baking sheet or transfer to a serving bowl.

Reason to Roast

Roasting vegetables is honestly one of the easiest ways to cook them with mega tasty results. Think about good roasted potatoes, which are tender on the inside and crispy on the outside. The key is to start with a hot oven (400°F or higher), be sure your vegetables are dry, and toss everything with olive oil and salt. You can roast so many vegetables using exactly the same method you use for the broccoli on page 104, including cauliflower, sweet potatoes, brussels sprouts, butternut squash, onions, fennel, eggplant, and bell peppers. The cooking times will vary depending on the vegetable, but as long as you cut all the pieces about the same size and keep your eye on the oven, turning the vegetables in the pan as needed, you can expect success.

Did You Know?

Cucumbers are mostly water (about 96 percent), so eating one is not a bad way to hydrate.

SPICY SWEET POTATO ROUNDS

Sweet potatoes are ridiculously versatile. You can cook them in a dozen different ways: cut into cubes to add to chili, grated along with cheese for quesadillas, and baked like a regular potato with a pat of butter slipped into the center. But far and away, this method of slicing and roasting sweet potatoes with olive oil and spices is my favorite. If you don't like spicy food, just leave out the cayenne pepper.

1 pound sweet potatoes, not peeled

2 tablespoons extra-virgin olive oil

1 teaspoon chili powder

½ teaspoon garlic powder

¼ teaspoon cayenne pepper (use more if you like things really spicy)

½ teaspoon kosher salt

KEY EQUIPMENT: cutting board, chef's knife, 2 large baking sheets, spatula

PRO TIP: Use these sweet potatoes in place of tortilla chips in Loaded Nachos on page 81.

Preheat oven to 400°F.

Wash and dry the sweet potatoes well. Put the sweet potatoes on a cutting board and use a chef's knife to cut them into rounds that are about ⅓-inch thick.

Pile the sliced sweet potatoes onto a large baking sheet and drizzle with olive oil. Use your hands to coat them in the oil. Sprinkle on the chili powder, garlic powder, cayenne pepper, and salt. Toss well, making sure the spices evenly coat all of the potato slices. Transfer half to a second baking sheet and spread them out so they're not crowded.

Bake for 15 minutes. Remove baking sheets from oven and use a spatula to flip them over. Return to the oven and cook until crisp and lightly browned (about 10 to 15 minutes more). Serve straight from the baking sheets or transfer to a bowl.

Make a Perfect Baked Potato

A simple baked potato is an excellent thing to know how to cook because it makes a great side dish or even a full meal when loaded up with favorite toppings. Here's how: Preheat the oven to 425°F. Wash and dry 1 russet potato. Stab the potato in several places with a paring knife. Use your hands to rub ½ teaspoon of olive oil over the potato and sprinkle with salt and a little black pepper. Put the potato on a baking sheet and bake until very tender on the inside and slightly crisp on the outside (you should be able to easily slide a paring knife into the center with little resistance). The potato will take about 1 hour, though the time will vary depending on its size and shape. Remove from oven and cut a slit lengthwise down the center. Tuck a slice of butter into the potato and add salt and pepper to taste or load it up with other toppings, such as chili, shredded Cheddar, crumbled bacon, steamed broccoli, cottage cheese, sour cream, or pickled jalapeños.

GARLICKY GREENS

When I use the term *greens* I'm usually referring to sturdy, dark leafy vegetables that are famously nutritious, such as collard greens, spinach, kale, and Swiss chard. When prepared well, they make for very good eating, particularly when tossed with garlic, butter, and balsamic vinegar. This recipe calls for kale, but the same technique can be applied to virtually any leafy green you'll find in the produce department.

1 bunch kale (any variety will work)

2 large cloves garlic

1 tablespoon extra-virgin olive oil

Pinch crushed red pepper flakes

¼ teaspoon kosher salt

½ tablespoon butter

½ teaspoon balsamic vinegar

KEY EQUIPMENT: cutting board, chef's knife, large skillet, tongs

PRO TIP: You can substitute collard greens, Swiss chard, beet greens, or spinach for kale. The cooking time will vary. More tender leaves, such as spinach, will cook very quickly. Heartier leaves, such as Swiss chard, will take longer.

Rinse the kale under running water and shake off the excess. Strip the leaves from the stems. Tear each leaf in a few pieces; discard the stems. Peel the garlic and thinly slice.

Set a large skillet on the stove over high heat. When it's good and hot, add the olive oil, garlic, and red pepper flakes. Stir the garlic for about 30 seconds, making sure it doesn't turn brown or burn.

Add as many of the torn greens as will comfortably fit in the pan. Use a pair of tongs or a fork to turn the kale until it wilts slightly. After about 30 seconds to 1 minute, when the greens have shrunk a little, add more kale and continue to sauté until all of the greens are in the pan. Add the salt and stir well.

Cook until the kale is tender and wilted (taste it to be sure). This will take a just few minutes. Remove pan from heat. Add the butter and drizzle with the balsamic vinegar. Gently stir to combine, melting the butter into the greens.

Serve right out of the cooking pan or transfer to a serving dish.

8 Easy Ways to Eat More Vegetables

Smoothies. Add 1 small handful of baby spinach, half of an avocado, or ¼ cup fresh or frozen cauliflower to your favorite fruit smoothie.

Pasta. Toss hot pasta with chopped cooked broccoli, cauliflower, asparagus, or peas, along with a big squeeze of lemon juice, olive oil, salt, pepper, and Parmesan cheese.

Scrambled eggs. Chop up leftover vegetables and stir them into scrambled eggs when they're nearly done.

Dips. Use raw, crunchy vegetables to scoop up guacamole, hummus, or onion dip instead of chips or crackers.

Quesadillas. Add grated cheese and an equal amount of any of the following to your quesadilla: raw baby spinach, grated raw zucchini or sweet potato, or a favorite chopped cooked vegetable.

Sandwiches. Include grated carrot, sliced cucumber, lettuce, tomato, avocado, sprouts, or bell peppers on your sandwiches and wraps.

Did You Know?
The most expensive fruit in the world is a Japanese variety of melon that once sold at auction for $23,000.

CILANTRO-LIME CORN

The flavors of this corn are borrowed from Mexico, where street cart vendors sell delicious corn on the cob seasoned with lime, cilantro, and other goodies. It's a brilliant combination and easy to pull off at home. If you happen to have a steaming basket on hand, by all means use it. Just nestle the basket in the pot, add the water, and lay the corn on top before covering it with a lid.

4 ears fresh corn

1 small bunch fresh cilantro

2 tablespoons butter

1 lime

Salt and black pepper to serve at the table

KEY EQUIPMENT: cutting board, chef's knife, large pot with lid, paring knife, tongs, small glass or ceramic bowl, microwave

PRO TIP: After buttering the corn, sprinkle 2 tablespoons crumbled cotija or grated Parmesan cheese over the 4 cobs.

Pull the husks and silks off the corn cobs and discard. Finely chop enough cilantro to fill 1 tablespoon.

Put enough water into a large pot so that it is ½-inch deep. Set the pot on the stove over high heat. When the water begins to simmer, lay the corn in the pot (it's okay if the cobs overlap or snap them in half nestle in a single layer).

Place the lid on the pot and steam the corn until done, about 5 to 7 minutes, turning the corn over halfway through. To test for doneness, lift a cob from the pot using a pair of tongs. Use a paring knife to wedge a kernel of corn off the cob and taste it. It should be sweet and a little crisp without that raw, starchy flavor.

While the corn cooks, put the butter into a small glass or ceramic bowl and microwave on high for 10 seconds to soften it. Add the cilantro and use a fork to mash it into the butter.

Put the cooked corn on a plate and spread the butter over the surface (you might need to use your hands for this). Use a chef's knife to cut the lime in half lengthwise. Cut each half into 3 wedges. Add to the plate with the corn.

Serve the corn while still warm. Add desired much salt, pepper, and lime juice.

Is Frozen as Good as Fresh?

Fresh is best—that's my general rule of thumb when it comes to fruits and vegetables. But I always keep a few frozen ones stashed in the freezer. Frozen produce is super convenient. Everything's already washed and cut, so it's less work when it comes time to cook. As for taste, it all depends on what you buy and how you use it:

- Frozen fruit is excellent for making smoothies. Frozen raspberries, bananas, wild blueberries, mangos, peaches, and pineapple do well in smoothies.
- Frozen grapes and raspberries make a refreshing snack (especially in the summer) straight from the freezer.
- Best bets for frozen vegetables? Frozen spinach, peas, and corn. I routinely add frozen spinach to my smoothies.
- Frozen broccoli, cauliflower, and butternut squash work great when used to make creamy, pureed soups.

Often though, the texture of vegetables just isn't the same once they've been frozen. When I'm blanching, steaming, or roasting vegetables, I use fresh when possible.

Choose Your Own Adventure:
VEGGIE TACOS

Meat and chicken may be typical taco fillings, but vegetables can be just as good. Start with a corn tortilla. Set a skillet over high heat, lightly coat it with oil, add the tortilla, and cook on one side until light brown and slightly crispy. Then fill the taco with favorite cooked vegetables and toppings. Here are 6 combos to get you started.

Corn tortilla

+

- sweet potato + black beans + Pepper Jack cheese
- corn + Cheddar cheese + cilantro
- zucchini + mushrooms + Cheddar cheese
- kale + avocado + pickled jalapeño
- avocado + chopped romaine hearts + Pepper Jack cheese

+

Taco toppings
lemon or lime juice
fresh cilantro
sour cream
grated cheese
guacamole
chopped lettuce or cabbage

+

Something spicy
Mexican salsa
sriracha
hot pepper sauce
pickled jalapeños

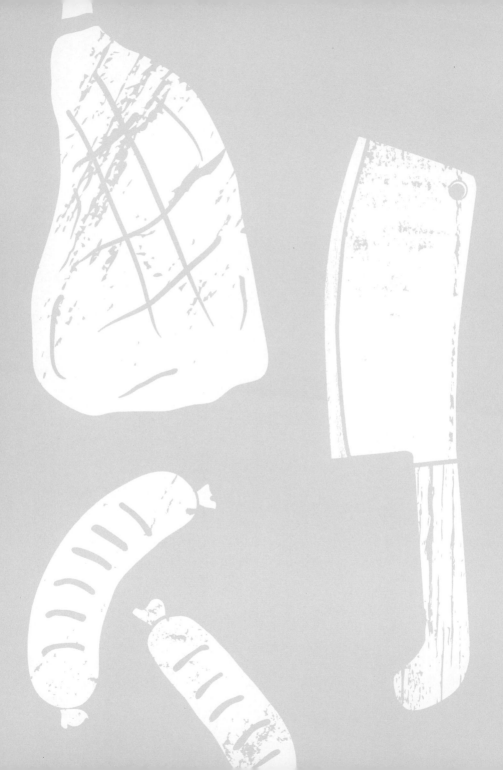

7 COOK MEAT, CHICKEN, AND FISH

Unless you're a vegetarian, you'll probably want to build some confidence around cooking meat, chicken, and fish. While it's not uncommon for newer cooks to be daunted by the idea of preparing these foods, it shouldn't be. With the right instruction and a little patience, it can be just as easy to cook a pork chop as a plate of pasta. Here are a few pointers:

Ask an expert. You have pros at the ready when you go to the supermarket: butchers and fishmongers. They can help you choose the freshest fish, advise on how much chicken to buy, or recommend the best way to cook a particular type of steak. Ask their advice.

Buy good ingredients. Buy the best quality meat, chicken, and fish that you can afford, even if it means eating it less often. Quality to me means meat and poultry that comes from a farm where they care about the animals; they let them roam and feed on their natural environment, and they don't overuse antibiotics. It's a level of quality that is not always easy to find and can be expensive, but raising animals this way is better for the environment, better for the animals, and tastes better on the plate.

Salt your food. Salt is everything when it comes to cooking animal protein. Chicken and meat usually benefit from being salted generously and in advance. Fish can be salted with a lighter hand and closer to the cooking time.

Don't overcook everything. Home cooks are often so afraid of undercooking meat and chicken that they overdo it. Learning to cook these foods just right is a matter of practice. At first you can rely on an instant-read thermometer to guide you. Eventually you'll know when to take a pork chop off the grill or a piece of salmon out of the pan just by look and feel.

LEMON-GARLIC CHICKEN THIGHS

Here's an insider tip when it comes to chicken: the thighs are where it's at. They're juicier, more flavorful, and also more forgiving to the cook (less likely to dry out), which is particularly good news for anyone new to the kitchen. Here, the thighs brown on the stove and then get finished in the oven. By the time they're done, a lemony sauce has pooled around them, which is excellent spooned over the finished dish.

4 bone-in, skin-on chicken thighs

¾ teaspoon kosher salt

Freshly ground black pepper

1 large lemon

3 large cloves garlic

2 teaspoons extra-virgin olive oil

¼ teaspoon dried thyme

⅓ cup chicken broth

KEY EQUIPMENT: chef's knife, cutting board, medium skillet with an ovenproof handle, tongs

Preheat oven to 425°F

Pat the chicken dry with paper towels. Sprinkle the salt over the surface of both sides of the chicken and use a pepper grinder to lightly shower it with pepper. Cut the lemon in half and squeeze enough juice to measure 3 tablespoons; set aside. Peel and chop the garlic and set aside.

Put a medium skillet on the stove over medium heat for 1 minute. Add the olive oil and let it heat up for about 30 seconds. Use tongs to lay the chicken thighs in the pan with the skin side down. Cook the chicken until the skin is golden brown, 6 to 7 minutes. Use tongs to turn the chicken over and cook on the second side for 3 minutes. Remove pan from heat and wait until the sizzling diminishes a bit, about 1 minute. Sprinkle the garlic and thyme into the pan. Add the broth and lemon juice.

Use a pot holder to transfer the pan to the oven. Cook until the chicken is done, about 15 minutes. Test for doneness by inserting an instant-read thermometer in the thickest part of the largest thigh. It's done when it reaches 165°F.

Serve chicken with juices spooned over the top.

SERVE WITH: Easy Brown Rice on page 45 is a good side dish for this chicken. Spoon the pan juices over the rice and serve a favorite cooked vegetable or salad on the side.

Cook with Caution

Cooking meat, chicken, and fish on the stove in a bit of oil is a very simple method that yields delicious results. The hot pan browns the outside while keeping things nice and tender on the inside. But there's one hitch: that hot oil can fly out of the pan and onto you if you aren't careful. A couple of tips:

- Don't drop food into the pan; lay it down gently to avoid causing the oil to splash out.
- Use tongs or a spatula with a long handle that will give your hand some distance from the pan.
- Use pot holders when maneuvering food in the pan.
- If you're an amateur, consider having a more experienced cook nearby when first learning to cook meat, chicken, or fish in a pan.

Did You Know?

According to the book *Tastes Like Chicken*, Americans eat 160 million servings of chicken a day.

CHEESEBURGERS WITH AWESOME SAUCE

MAKES 4 BURGERS

It's easy to pick up an ordinary burger at your local drive-through, but with a little extra effort, you can make a truly excellent one yourself. Here are a few secrets to success: First, buy lean as opposed to extra-lean burger meat. You want some fat in your burgers because that's part of what makes them juicy, so look for beef that's about 85 percent lean or 15 percent fat. Second, don't beat the heck out of the meat when you make the patties. That will turn your burgers tough, not tender. Third, salt the surface generously to brighten the flavor. Lastly, slather on the Awesome Sauce. It's the crowning touch.

1⅓ pounds lean ground beef

1 heaping teaspoon kosher salt

Freshly ground black pepper

2 tablespoons ketchup

3 tablespoons mayonnaise

½ teaspoon Dijon mustard

Nonstick cooking spray

4 thin slices sharp Cheddar cheese

4 soft hamburger buns or English muffins

8 dill pickle slices

4 thin slices red onion

4 crunchy lettuce leaves, such as romaine

KEY EQUIPMENT: small bowl, large heavy skillet (such as a 12-inch cast-iron one), spatula, toaster

Divide the ground beef into 4 equal pieces and gently roll each one into a ball as you would a ball of clay. Pat each ball into a hamburger patty that is about ¾-inch thick and 4 inches in diameter. Do your best to make the burgers evenly thick across the entire burger. Sprinkle half the salt over the burgers. Use a pepper grinder to add a light shower of pepper to the top of the burgers. Turn the burgers over and sprinkle on the remaining salt and a little more pepper.

Make the Awesome Sauce by mixing together the ketchup, mayonnaise, and mustard with a fork in a small bowl until smooth.

Set a large skillet over high heat for 1 to 2 minutes until the pan sizzles when you flick a bit of water into it. Lightly coat the pan with nonstick cooking spray and set the burgers in the pan. Cook for 3 minutes. Use a spatula to turn the burgers over (being careful to avoid the spray of the hot grease in the skillet). Immediately lay a piece of cheese on top of

each burger and cook until medium rare, another 3 minutes. It should be pink in the center but no longer raw looking. (You can poke a paring knife into the center and have a peek.) For a medium or medium-well burger, cook an additional 1 to 1½ minutes.

While the burgers cook, split the buns in half and lightly toast them.

To assemble, use a spatula to transfer the burgers to the bottom half of the buns. Lay the pickles, onion, and lettuce on top. Spread Awesome Sauce on the inside of the top bun and cover burgers.

Serve immediately

SERVE WITH: Spicy Sweet Potato Rounds on page 107.

Did You Know?

If you lined up in a row all the hamburgers Americans eat each year, it would circle the globe more than 32 times.

SKILLET SKIRT STEAK
WITH HERB BUTTER

MAKES 4 SERVINGS

Skirt steak is an ideal starter steak for beginner cooks. That's because it's thin and nicely marbled with fat, which means it cooks quickly with lots of built-in flavor. Frankly, it's hard to mess up. Even if you overcook it slightly, it will still be tasty. Serve the steak seasoned with just salt and pepper or slather on the herb butter. See how the buttery chives and capers brighten all the flavors as they melt onto the meat.

1¼ pounds skirt steak

1 teaspoon kosher salt, plus 1 pinch

Freshly ground black pepper

3 tablespoons butter

1 small bundle fresh chives

1½ tablespoons capers

½ teaspoon lemon juice

2 teaspoons canola oil

KEY EQUIPMENT: small glass or ceramic bowl, microwave, cutting board, chef's knife, large heavy skillet (ideally cast-iron), tongs

Remove the steak from the fridge 30 minutes before you plan to cook, and season on both sides with 1 teaspoon salt and a light dusting of black pepper.

While the meat rests, make the Herb Butter. Take the butter out of the fridge and put it into a small glass or ceramic bowl. Microwave on high for 8 seconds to soften. Put the chives on a cutting board and use a chef's knife to mince enough to fill 1 tablespoon. Add the chives, capers, lemon juice, pinch of salt, and a few grinds of pepper to the butter. Use a fork to mash everything together into a smooth consistency. Set aside.

Pull out a large skillet, big enough for the steak to lay flat. If your pan is too small, cut the steak in half crosswise to fit the pan.

Set the pan on the stove over high heat and add the canola oil. As the oil heats up, tilt the pan so it coats bottom (use a pot holder to protect your hand). When the pan is good and hot, add the steak and cook for about 3 minutes, or until nicely browned on one side. Use a pair of tongs to flip it over, and continue to cook until lightly browned, about 3 minutes more for medium-rare.

You can check to see if it's done by making a little slit in the center with a paring knife and peeking inside. For medium-rare, it should be pink but no longer bloody. For medium or medium-well, cook an additional 1 to 2 minutes.

Use a pair of tongs to transfer the meat to a cutting board and let it rest for 5 minutes.

Cut the steak across the grain (opposite the directional lines you see in the meat) in 1-inch-wide pieces. Arrange the herb butter in a line down the center of the steak so every slice gets a bit of butter. Serve immediately.

SERVE WITH: Baked potatoes, see page 108, and Chopped Greek Salad on page 89.

How Do You Like Your Meat?

An instant-read thermometer is a slender tool that gives a quick read on the internal temperature of food. It's handy for determining if your meat or chicken is cooked enough. Every kitchen should have one. You can gauge the temperature by spearing the pointy end of the thermometer into the center of the meat or chicken. Aim for the thickest part and avoid contact with any bones.

MAPLE-MUSTARD PORK CHOPS

MAKES 2 SERVINGS

Pork chops are handy because you can go to your butcher and buy just a single chop for yourself or several if you're cooking for friends. You can pare this recipe down to the bare bones (no pun intended), skipping the maple-mustard sauce and serving each chop with a big spoonful of store-bought applesauce instead. A classic.

2 bone-in pork chops, each about 8 ounces and 1-inch thick

½ teaspoon kosher salt

Freshly ground black pepper

2 tablespoons whole grain Dijon mustard (sold in jars near the regular Dijon mustard)

1 tablespoon pure maple syrup

1 tablespoon sour cream

1 teaspoon apple cider vinegar

1 tablespoon canola oil

KEY EQUIPMENT: large heavy skillet (cast-iron is ideal), small bowl, tongs, instant-read thermometer

Put the pork chops on a plate and sprinkle both sides with the salt. Use a pepper grinder to generously coat both sides with black pepper. Leave the chops to rest at room temperature for 30 minutes.

While the chops rest, make the sauce in a small bowl by mixing together the mustard, maple syrup, sour cream, and apple cider vinegar. Set aside.

Put a heavy skillet large enough to fit both chops on the stove over high heat. Leave it for 2 to 3 minutes, to get very hot. Add the canola oil to the pan, drop the heat to medium, and tilt the pan so the oil coats the bottom (use a pot holder to protect your hand). Carefully lay the chops in the pan (don't drop them in, otherwise the oil will splatter). Cook until nicely browned on the first side, 5 minutes. Use tongs to turn the chops over, laying them down gently. Cook on the other side until an instant-read thermometer measures 140°F in the fattest part of the chops, measuring in a couple of places. This will take another 5 to 6 minutes. The time will vary depending on the size of the chops, the temperature, and the pan.

> **PRO TIP:** Make a side of sautéed apples to go with the pork chops by cutting 1 medium apple into very thin slices. When you remove the cooked chops from the pan, add the apple slices and a big pinch of salt. Sauté the apples over medium heat, stirring regularly, until slightly tender, 2 to 3 minutes. Spoon onto the plate with the pork chops.

Use the tongs to transfer the chops to a clean plate. Let rest for 5 minutes. Spoon a little sauce over the top and serve with extra sauce on the side.

SERVE WITH: Garlicky Greens on page 109 and the sautéed apples described in the Pro Tip.

Carryover Cooking

Here's something you need to know: food keeps cooking even after it's off the heat. For example, if you cook a steak to a perfect medium-rare and then take it off the grill to rest, it will keep on cooking. When it comes time to carve into your meat, it may be cooked more than you want. That's called carryover cooking and is something to keep in mind when you're cooking meat, chicken, or fish on the stove, in the oven, or on the grill.

EASY TERIYAKI SALMON

If you like teriyaki chicken, you'll probably like teriyaki salmon, too—even if you're not a huge fan of fish. The sweet and salty sauce is an easy way to add lots of flavor with very little effort.

4 salmon fillets, about 5 to 6 ounces each (see note)

¾ teaspoon kosher salt

⅛ teaspoon black pepper

4 green onions

2 teaspoons canola oil

3 tablespoons teriyaki sauce (sold in the Asian foods section of the market)

2 teaspoons sesame seeds

KEY EQUIPMENT: cutting board, chef's knife, large heavy skillet, spatula

Use a paper towel to blot the moisture from the salmon fillets. Sprinkle the salt and pepper over both sides of the fish.

Lay the green onions on a cutting board. Trim off the hairy-looking tips and dark green ends and discard. Cut the white and light green parts into thin, crosswise slices.

Put a large, heavy skillet over high heat and add the oil. When the oil is good and hot, swirl it around to coat the bottom of the pan (use pot holders to protect your hand). Lay the salmon fillets with the skin side down in the pan. Turn the heat down to medium. As the fish cooks, the color will gradually turn paler and more opaque starting at the bottom and moving up. When that lighter color has moved about halfway up side of the fish and the bottom is crisp, use a spatula to turn over the fillets. (This initial cooking time for the first side will vary from 3 to 5 minutes, depending on the thickness of the fish.)

Cook the other side another 3 to 5 minutes, until the flesh of the fish parts easily if you insert a paring knife. The color in the center should be nearly opaque.

Use a spatula to transfer the fish to a serving plate with the skin side down. Immediately spoon the teriyaki sauce over the top of the fish. Sprinkle with the chopped green onions and sesame seeds.

SERVE WITH: Easy Brown Rice on page 45 and Japanese Cucumber Salad on page 92.

NOTE: Salmon has little bones that run along the center of the fillet. If you poke your finger along the fish you will feel them. You can use a pair of tweezers or pliers to pull them out before you cook. Also, if your market only sells salmon in large pieces rather than individual fillets, you can ask for a piece of salmon that's about 1½ pounds and ask the butcher to cut it into 4 fillets for you (or you can cut it yourself at home using a chef's knife).

Choose Your Own Adventure:
SCRUMPTIOUS SANDWICHES

Leftover chicken, steak, fish, and pork are prime fixings for building delicious sandwiches. All that's needed is bread of some kind and anything you like to layer in between.

Choose a bread
whole wheat, baguette, Dutch crunch, sliced levain, rye, multigrain, sourdough

Add leftovers
sliced steak, chicken, meatballs, pork, or fish

Slather on a spread
mayonnaise, mustard, pesto, butter, tartar sauce, tapenade, hummus

Choose a cheese
Cheddar, Monterey Jack, Swiss, Gruyere, blue cheese, cream cheese, goat cheese

Add veggies and greens
tomato, lettuce, arugula, baby kale, spinach, cucumber, avocado, roasted red peppers, artichoke hearts

Boost the flavor
salt, pepper, hot chilies, lemon juice, pickles, balsamic vinegar

8 MAKE SNACKS AND LITTLE MEALS

It's 2 hours until dinner and you're starving. You don't want to totally wreck your appetite, but you need something to tide you over. This is where snacks and little meals come in: lighter bites that are easy and inexpensive to make. Nothing is too fussy because who wants to labor over a simple snack? In fact, everything in this chapter can be done in about 5 minutes or less.

You'll find 5 ideas here that run the gamut from yogurt sundaes to a super easy pizza. They're the kind of recipes that will come in handy when you're off to college or in your first apartment without much in the way of cooking tools or extra cash. You can always make a little meal.

LOADED PEANUT BUTTER TOAST

Toast is an excellent starting point upon which to build a little meal. Add peanut butter and you have something that will fill your belly. Lay down slices of strawberries and banana and it goes from plain to pretty. Finish with a drizzle of honey and a dash of cinnamon and your simple slice of toast is now a snack you'll want to make on repeat.

1 slice whole grain bread

1 heaping tablespoon peanut butter

1 teaspoon honey

2 medium strawberries, stems removed

⅓ banana

Dash cinnamon

1 teaspoon sesame seeds, chia seeds, or hemp seeds (optional)

KEY EQUIPMENT: toaster, paring knife

PRO TIP: Use any nut or seed butter in place of peanut butter, such as almond, cashew, sunflower, pumpkin seed, or soy nut butter.

Toast the bread. Spread peanut butter on top of the toast and drizzle with honey. Use a paring knife to cut the strawberries and banana into thin slices and lay them in rows along the toast. Sprinkle cinnamon and seeds over the top. Dig in.

SERVE WITH: A glass of cold milk.

Better Nut Butter

The healthiest nut butters are typically made with the fewest ingredients. I also happen to think they taste the best. One downside, though, is that the oil from the nuts can separate, so you may see a pool of oil on top when you open the jar. Here's a quick fix: store the jar upside down. Then when you turn it right side up to open it, the creamy nut butter will be waiting for you at the top.

YOGURT SUNDAE WITH MELTED RASPBERRIES

Let's be honest, this isn't really a sundae because everyone knows that would require ice cream. But it's so good, calling it a sundae doesn't feel like a stretch. You might be surprised to know that this recipe works best with frozen, not fresh, raspberries. They get really juicy when defrosted, which makes an excellent sauce poured over yogurt.

⅓ cup frozen raspberries

¾ cup plain Greek yogurt

½ teaspoon pure maple syrup (more if you like it sweeter)

1 tablespoon granola

1 tablespoon chopped walnuts, almonds, or hazelnuts

KEY EQUIPMENT: 2 small glass or ceramic bowls, microwave

PRO TIP: This is a good one to pack into a container and take on the go for a light meal or snack.

Put the berries in a small glass or ceramic bowl. Microwave on high for 1 minute. If you don't have a microwave, heat in a small saucepan on the stove over medium heat until warm and juicy. Put the yogurt into another small bowl, like a cereal bowl, and pour the warm berries over the top, followed by the maple syrup. Sprinkle the granola and nuts over the berries. Enjoy with a spoon.

Greek or Regular Yogurt: What's Better?

Neither. They're just different. Greek yogurt is thicker than regular yogurt because some of the liquid (whey) gets strained off. As a result, Greek yogurt has more protein but regular yogurt has more calcium. Both have their place in the kitchen.

20 Easy Ideas for Lighter Bites

1. Hummus with vegetables
2. A bowl of cereal with sliced banana
3. Tuna salad on crackers
4. Black beans with cheese and salsa
5. A bowl of oatmeal (see recipe, page 40)
6. Half an avocado with a squeeze of lemon and pinch of salt (eat with a spoon)
7. A smoothie made with 1 seedless tangerine, ½ cup milk, ½ cup vanilla yogurt, 2 ice cubes
8. A fried egg on a tortilla with salsa
9. Carrot sticks and almond butter
10. A bowl of ramen soup
11. Scrambled eggs with a handful of baby spinach
12. Turkey and cheese rolled inside of a tortilla
13. Celery topped with peanut butter
14. Half of a favorite sandwich
15. Applesauce topped with yogurt
16. Avocado toast
17. Peanut butter on graham crackers
18. Tomato soup and crackers
19. Yogurt with berries and granola
20. Half of a bagel with cream cheese, cucumber, and tomato

QUICK-FIX PITA PIZZA

MAKES 1 SMALL PIZZA

If you ever feel inclined to learn the art and science of making really excellent pizza with homemade dough, go for it. In the meantime, this Pita Pizza can hold you over. It will take no more than 3 minutes to assemble and bakes up into a cheesy pie with a crispy crust that will satisfy a pizza craving any time of day or night.

2 tablespoons marinara or pizza sauce

1 seven-inch pita bread

½ heaping cup shredded mozzarella cheese

Any favorite pizza toppings, such as sliced mushrooms, salami, arugula, fresh basil, bell peppers, or cherry tomatoes

KEY EQUIPMENT: cheese grater, baking sheet, cutting board, chef's knife

PRO TIP: Make 2 and stash the extra one in the fridge to reheat for tomorrow's breakfast or lunch.

Preheat oven or toaster oven to 400°F.

Spread the marinara sauce over the surface of the pita bread, leaving a ⅓-inch border around the edge. Sprinkle the mozzarella over the marinara sauce. Add toppings.

Put the pita on a baking sheet and bake in the oven or toaster oven until the cheese melts and the bottom is crispy, about 8 minutes.

Remove from oven. Put on a cutting board and use a chef's knife to cut into quarters.

TRUE-BLUE SMOOTHIE

MAKES 1 SMOOTHIE

Everyone should have a good smoothie recipe up their sleeve. Why? Because it's the sort of thing you can make with just a few ingredients that tastes good and is pretty darn good for you. This one is creamy, slightly sweet, and delicious enough that you might mistake it for a shake. You can bump up the nutrition by adding a small handful of baby spinach to the blender. If you have a straw on hand, use it. I swear smoothies taste better sipped through a straw.

½ cup plain yogurt

½ cup milk (cow's milk or plant milk, such as almond or soy)

½ cup fresh or frozen blueberries

½ ripe banana

2 teaspoons pure maple syrup

½ teaspoon vanilla extract

2 ice cubes

KEY EQUIPMENT: blender

PRO TIP: For even creamier smoothies, freeze your bananas before adding to the blender. To do so, let bananas get good and ripe (the peel should be speckled brown). Then peel and put them into a resealable freezer bag. They will last for several months in the freezer.

Put all the ingredients into a blender and blend until creamy and smooth. Pour into a tall glass and serve.

Turn Smoothies into Freezer Pops

If you've got leftovers in the blender after you make a smoothie, pour into ice pop molds and freeze. You'll have a tasty frozen treat.

GUACAMOLE

Once you've made your own guacamole at home, you'll wonder why anyone would ever buy it at the store. It's one of the easiest and most universally popular dips out there. Serve it with your favorite crunchy vegetables or tortilla chips, and you've got a satisfying snack on your hands.

1 small red or yellow onion

¼ teaspoon kosher salt

⅛ teaspoon black pepper

1 lime

1 large ripe avocado

1½ to 2 cups cut-up raw vegetables such as carrots, cucumbers, and red bell peppers and/or tortilla chips for dipping

KEY EQUIPMENT: cutting board, chef's knife, small bowl

PRO TIP: If you make guacamole ahead of time, lay a piece of plastic wrap right on the surface of the dip to keep it from turning brown, and store in the fridge.

Dice enough onion to measure 1 tablespoon and put into a small bowl with the salt and pepper. Cut the lime in half and squeeze enough juice to fill 2 teaspoons. Pour the lime juice over the onions.

Scoop out the flesh of the avocado and add it to the onion. Use a fork to mash and stir the avocado until nearly smooth and evenly blended with the other ingredients. Serve with cut-up vegetables and/or tortilla chips.

How to Ripen an Avocado

Avocados don't ripen on the tree; they ripen after they've been picked. To make really good guacamole, you need ripe avocados. To hurry up the process, put an avocado in a brown paper bag with an apple or banana (the fruit will hasten the ripening). Close the bag and store for 2 to 3 days, by which time the avocado should be ready. A ripe avocado will dent with relative ease when pressed with your thumb.

Stove-Top Buttered Popcorn

Making popcorn from scratch rather than buying it is seriously better and cheaper—not to mention that it has none of the chemicals in microwavable bags. Here's how: Put a medium-size pot with a lid on the stove over medium-high heat. Add 1 tablespoon olive oil and ⅓ cup popcorn kernels. Cover with a lid and wait until you hear the first kernel pop. Hold on to the pan handle (use a pot holder if needed) and give it a vigorous shake to distribute the popcorn. Continue to cook, shaking the pot every 15 to 30 seconds, until the popping slows to just an occasional pop. Remove from heat and transfer to a large bowl. Put 2 tablespoons butter into a small glass or ceramic dish and microwave on high until melted, about 1 minute. Drizzle over the popcorn and add ½ teaspoon kosher salt. Toss well. Makes 6½ cups.

Did You Know?
Avocados are a fruit, not a vegetable.

Choose Your Own Adventure:
TOAST BAR

A slice of your favorite bread is an ideal base to create a mini meal that can be sweet or savory, healthy or decadent, lean and mean, or piled high. Here are a slew of ideas to get you started.

Choose a bread
whole wheat, white, baguette, levain, rye, bagel, English muffin, pita, seed, multigrain

Toast the bread

Add a spread
hummus, peanut butter, almond butter, sunbutter, cream cheese, goat cheese, ricotta cheese, Nutella, jam, tahini, avocado

Add 1 or more toppings
chopped nuts: almonds, walnuts, cashews, hazelnuts, pecans
dried fruits: raisins, chopped dates, chopped apricots, cranberries
seeds: sunflower seeds, pepitas, hemp seeds, flax seeds, chia seeds
fruit: whole raspberries or blueberries or sliced strawberries, banana, peach, pear, or apple
vegetables: sliced cucumber, sliced radish, grated carrot, sliced tomato, spinach, arugula
protein: bacon, prosciutto, ham, turkey, smoked salmon, salami, egg, feta cheese, goat cheese, Parmesan cheese, Cheddar cheese

Add flavor boosters
salt, black pepper, lemon juice, hot pepper sauce, balsamic vinegar, olive oil, cayenne pepper, chili powder, cinnamon, honey, cumin, chives, basil, mint, lime juice, salsa

9 FEED YOUR FRIENDS

High on the list of reasons to cook is so that you can spoil your friends and family with good food. Of course, your buddies are perfectly capable of feeding themselves, but it's pretty satisfying to make something totally delicious to share. Sitting around a table over a meal is as good a way to be with the people you like as anything I know, so why not learn to cook share-worthy food?

One factor I look for when it comes to cooking for others is to find recipes that I can make ahead of time. I like to do most of my prep in advance so I'm not stuck in the kitchen when everyone arrives. The recipes in this chapter all meet this requirement.

BAKED MAC AND CHEESE

MAKES 6 SERVINGS

What's not to love about a big pan of mac and cheese, hot from the oven, teeming with melted Cheddar and crowned with a buttery topping? Pretty much nothing. This recipe may not be as quick as making mac and cheese from a box, but it's worth every minute. Warning: it's practically impossible *not* to pick at the addictive golden crust on top.

Nonstick cooking spray

1 teaspoon kosher salt, plus more for salting the pasta cooking water

16 ounces rotini or fusilli pasta

8 ounces sharp Cheddar cheese

2 cups milk

One 16-ounce container cottage cheese (2 cups)

¼ teaspoon cayenne pepper

¼ teaspoon black pepper

3 tablespoons finely grated Parmesan cheese

¼ cup plain breadcrumbs, such as Progresso brand

1 tablespoon butter

KEY EQUIPMENT: 8- or 9-inch square baking pan, large pot, cheese grater, colander, baking sheet, blender

Preheat oven to 375°F. Grease an 8- or 9-inch square baking pan with nonstick cooking spray.

Fill a large pot with water and add enough salt so that the water tastes slightly salty. Put on the stove over high heat and bring to a boil. Add the pasta and cook according to package directions until al dente (see page 56).

While the pasta cooks, grate the Cheddar cheese and set aside.

Put the milk, cottage cheese, cayenne, salt, and pepper into a blender and blend until creamy, about 30 seconds.

When the pasta is done, drain it well in a colander set in the sink. Immediately put the drained pasta back into the pot and add the blended milk–cottage cheese mixture. Set aside 1 cup of the grated Cheddar (you'll use this on top later). Add the rest of the grated Cheddar to the pasta. Stir until the cheese melts and blends into a creamy sauce. If the heat of the pot isn't enough to melt everything, set the pot over low heat and stir until creamy and melted.

PRO TIP: This is a great dish to get into the oven just as your friends show up so that it's done by the time you're ready to eat.

Transfer the pasta to the prepared baking pan. It may be right up to the very top. Sprinkle the remaining 1 cup of grated Cheddar evenly on top, followed by the Parmesan and the breadcrumbs. Cut the butter into tiny, thin slivers and place them on top of the breadcrumbs.

Put the mac and cheese on a large baking sheet (in case some of the cheese sauce bubbles over) and bake until golden across the top, about 35 minutes.

Remove from the oven and serve.

SERVE WITH: Roasted Broccoli with Lemon and Parmesan on page 104 or Buttery Green Beans on page 102.

Did You Know?

When Kraft first came out with mac and cheese in 1937, it cost nineteen cents a box, less than a nickel a serving.

SHEET-PAN CHICKEN AND POTATOES

MAKES 8 PIECES OF CHICKEN, 4 TO 6 SERVINGS

Roasting a whole chicken is easy; the tricky part is carving it. Luckily with this recipe there's no carving required because you roast just the thighs and legs. Cooking the potatoes in the same pan means all the delicious chicken drippings drift onto the spuds and make them seriously tender and tasty. Try to salt the chicken a day or two before you cook it; you'll get a much more flavorful bird.

4 bone-in, skin-on chicken thighs, (see note)

4 bone-in, skin-on chicken legs, (see note)

2½ teaspoons kosher salt, divided

1 lemon

1 teaspoon smoked paprika

½ teaspoon black pepper

2 pounds small red, white, or Yukon Gold potatoes

1 tablespoon extra-virgin olive oil

3 cloves garlic

Several large sprigs fresh rosemary

KEY EQUIPMENT: cutting board, chef's knife, large baking sheet with sides, spatula, instant-read thermometer, tongs, pastry brush

Put the chicken in a pan that's just large enough to accommodate it and sprinkle 2 teaspoons of salt over it. If time allows, cover loosely with plastic wrap and refrigerate for 1 to 2 days. Remove from the refrigerator 30 minutes before you plan to cook.

Preheat oven to 400°F.

Cut the lemon in half and squeeze the juices over the chicken. Sprinkle the paprika and black pepper evenly over the surface of the chicken.

Wash and dry the potatoes. Cut them into quarters and put on a large baking sheet with sides. Drizzle the olive oil over the potatoes, sprinkle on the remaining ½ teaspoon salt and use your hands to toss everything together. Nestle the chicken pieces among the potatoes and spread everything out over the baking sheet.

Peel and thinly slice the garlic. Chop enough fresh rosemary leaves to fill 2 tablespoons. Sprinkle the garlic and chopped rosemary over the chicken and potatoes.

Bake for 25 minutes. Remove the pan from the oven and use a spatula to move the potatoes around a bit. Use a pastry brush to mop up some of the liquid from the pan and brush it on the chicken, so it's moist and glossy. If you don't

NOTE: Chicken legs and thighs are often sold as 1 piece. Ask the butcher at your market to separate the legs from the thighs, so you have 8 pieces total.

have a pastry brush, use a spoon to scoop up the juices to pour over the chicken. Return to the oven.

Bake another 10 minutes and then begin checking to see if the chicken is done by inserting an instant-read thermometer into the center of the largest chicken thigh. It's done when it reaches 165°F (check in a few places to be sure).

When the chicken is done, remove the baking sheet from the oven and use a pair of tongs to transfer the chicken to a serving platter. Put the potatoes back into the oven and continue to cook until they are very tender when you insert a knife in the center and are golden brown, an additional 10 to 15 minutes or so.

Transfer the cooked potatoes to the platter with the chicken. Carefully lift the baking pan and tilt it over the chicken and potatoes to drizzle on the juices.

SERVE WITH: Green Salad with Shake-It-Up Dressing on page 86 and/or Garlicky Greens on page 109.

10 Good Things to Cook for Friends and Family

1. Softly Scrambled Eggs (page 26). Great for when friends sleep over and everyone wakes up hungry.
2. Green Goodness Dressing (page 93). Make a batch and put it out with a big plate of cut-up vegetables, such as carrots, celery, cherry tomatoes, and cucumbers for dipping.
3. One-Bowl Chocolate Chip Cookies (page 165). Especially just warm from the oven with glasses of cold milk.
4. Pasta with Butter, Egg, and Cheese (page 57). Even your picky friends just might go for it.
5. Loaded Nachos (page 81). Especially good for game day or movie night.
6. Golden Banana Bread (page 162). Perfect to wrap up and deliver as a "Thank you," I'm sorry," or "Feel better."
7. True-Blue Smoothie (page 139). A quick fix for an afternoon snack.
8. Vanilla Cupcakes with Fudgy Frosting (page 170). Exactly what you need for friends with birthdays.
9. Breakfast Burritos (page 74). Good for lunch and dinner, too.
10. Chopped Greek Salad (page 89). This salad might make converts of even veggie-phobic friends.

HOMEMADE SAUCY MEATBALLS

Meatballs are always a big hit, which is why this recipe is one I make again and again when friends come to dinner. I don't serve them the traditional way, over heaps of spaghetti. Instead, I spoon the meatballs into shallow bowls with just tomato sauce for company. There's always plenty of Parmesan to grate over the top and a crusty loaf of Italian bread to scoop up every last bit of goodness. Nobody is ever disappointed.

½ cup Italian bread crumbs (such as the Progresso brand)

½ cup milk

1 small bunch Italian parsley

½ cup finely grated Parmesan cheese, plus more to pass at the table

2 teaspoons dried oregano

2 teaspoons garlic powder

1 egg

½ pound spicy Italian sausage (uncooked sausage)

1 pound lean ground beef

1 double batch of Genius Tomato Sauce on page 54 (see note)

1 loaf Italian bread or baguette

Preheat oven to 375°F. Lay a piece of aluminum foil or parchment paper on a large baking sheet with sides.

Put the breadcrumbs into a large bowl and pour the milk over the top. Soak the breadcrumbs in the milk for 1 minute. Put the parsley on the cutting board and finely chop enough leaves to fill ¼ cup. Save the remaining parsley for another use.

Add the chopped parsley, Parmesan, oregano, garlic, and egg to the breadcrumbs and stir thoroughly.

Use a paring knife to slit the thin casing of the sausage open from end to end. Turn the casing inside out and empty the sausage meat into the bowl with the breadcrumbs. Discard the casing. Add the ground beef to the bowl and gently but thoroughly blend all the ingredients together so everything is evenly mixed. (I use my hands to do the mixing.) Try not to be too aggressive or it will make your meatballs tough.

Pinch off ¼ cup of the meat mixture, roll it into a ball in the palms of your hands, and put on the baking sheet. Continue with the remaining meat, spacing the meatballs evenly on the baking sheet. You should have about

KEY EQUIPMENT:

aluminum foil or parchment paper, large baking sheet with sides, large bowl, cheese grater, cutting board, chef's knife, can opener

NOTE: Make a double batch of the Genius Tomato Sauce on page 54, which means you will need two 28-ounce cans tomatoes, 2 onions, ½ cup butter, 2 teaspoons salt, and ½ cup chopped fresh basil.

PRO TIP: If you want to serve this over spaghetti, you'll need about 24 ounces of pasta to serve 8 people (One and a half 16-ounce boxes). Cook it in a large pot of boiling water according to package directions. Drain well, stir a few teaspoons of olive oil into the pasta so it doesn't stick together, and serve with the meatballs and sauce on top.

14 meatballs. Bake until cooked through in the center and lightly browned, about 30 minutes.

While the meatballs bake, make a double batch of the Genius Tomato Sauce. Once sauce and meatballs are done, transfer the meatballs from the baking sheet into the sauce.

To serve, put a big spoonful of sauce and a couple of meatballs into serving bowls (about the size of a cereal bowl). Serve with thick slices of bread. Have extra Parmesan at the table in case anyone wants to sprinkle it on top.

SERVE WITH: Arugula Salad with Balsamic Vinaigrette on page 91.

THAI-STYLE COCONUT CURRY NOODLE SOUP

MAKES 4 TO 5 SERVINGS

This soup is a good bet for when you're cooking for vegetarian and vegan friends. That said, you certainly don't have to be a vegetarian to love it, packed as it is with rich coconut curry flavor. Tender rice noodles make it plenty filling, too.

1 medium yellow onion

2 cloves garlic

3 large carrots

6 ounces white or cremini mushrooms

1 medium zucchini

6 ounces extra-firm tofu

2 teaspoons canola oil

One 13½-ounce can coconut milk (see note)

3½ cups low-sodium vegetable broth

2 tablespoons red curry paste (see note)

1 firmly packed tablespoon brown sugar

2 tablespoons Asian fish sauce (see note)

1 teaspoon kosher salt

(continued)

Finely chop the onion and garlic. Peel the carrots, trim off the root end, and cut into ¼-inch-thick slices. Cut the mushrooms into ¼-inch-thick slices. Trim the ends of the zucchini, cut it in half lengthwise, and cut into ¼-inch-thick slices (like half-moons). Cut the tofu into ½-inch cubes.

Put a large pot with a lid on the stove over medium-high heat and add the oil. When the pan is hot, add the onion and sauté, stirring regularly, until tender, about 5 minutes. Add the garlic and continue to sauté, 1 minute.

Add the coconut milk, broth, curry paste, brown sugar, fish sauce, and salt. Turn the heat to high and stir until the ingredients blend. Add the carrots, mushrooms, zucchini, and tofu. Stir, and turn the heat to high. When the soup boils, drop the heat until it simmers. Simmer until the carrots are just tender, about 6 minutes.

While the soup simmers, cook the noodles by filling a medium pot with water and bringing it to a boil over high heat. When the water boils, cook the noodles according to package directions. When done, drain in a colander set in the sink. Rinse with cold water and set aside.

6 ounces Asian pad Thai rice noodles (dried noodles that are long and flat, like fettuccine)

2 limes

2 large handfuls baby spinach

¼ cup roughly chopped cilantro

KEY EQUIPMENT: cutting board, chef's knife, vegetable peeler, large heavy pot with a lid, medium pot, soup ladle

NOTE: These ingredients are sold in the Asian section of supermarkets, in specialty markets, and online.

PRO TIP: If you like your soup really spicy, add another teaspoon of curry paste or serve with sriracha at the table to add as desired.

When the carrots are tender, squeeze enough lime juice to fill 2 tablespoons and add to the soup. Add the spinach. Stir well.

To serve, divide the noodles among serving bowls and ladle the soup over the top. Garnish with cilantro leaves.

Did You Know?

Canned coconut milk is a different thing entirely from the coconut milk sold as a beverage alongside soy, almond, and rice milk. It's thicker and richer, used more for cooking and baking than drinking.

BIG POT OF TURKEY CHILI

A heaping pot of smoky, not-too-spicy chili is an excellent way to feed your friends. Also a plus is that you can do all of the cooking ahead of time, so you don't have to lift a finger once they show up. It also happens to be seriously tasty, especially topped with a spoonful of sour cream. Hopefully there will be leftovers because you'll want to eat this again.

3 slices bacon

1 large onion

1 large clove garlic

1½ pounds ground turkey

1 chipotle pepper en adobo

1 tablespoon chili powder

1¼ teaspoons ground cumin

1 teaspoon paprika

1¼ teaspoons kosher salt

One 28-ounce can crushed tomatoes

2½ cups low-sodium chicken broth

Two 14½-ounce cans pinto beans

1 cup fresh or frozen corn kernels (no need to defrost)

¾ cup sour cream for serving

Lay the bacon in a stack on a cutting board and cut crosswise into ½-inch-wide pieces. Chop the onion. Peel the garlic and cut into very thin slices.

Set a large pot over medium heat. Add the bacon and cook, stirring regularly, for 1 minute. Add the onion and sauté until tender and translucent, stirring regularly, about 5 minutes. Increase the heat to medium-high and add the garlic and ground turkey. Cook until the turkey is no longer pink in the center, stirring regularly with a spoon to break up the turkey so it looks like taco meat, about 6 minutes.

Put the chipotle pepper on a cutting board and chop it until it turns into a smooth paste. Add to the pot along with the chili powder, cumin, paprika, and salt. Stir well. Add the tomatoes and chicken broth and stir again. Put a lid on the pot and drop the heat to low. Cook for 25 minutes.

Open the cans of beans and pour into a colander in the sink to drain the liquid. Add the beans and corn to the chili. Adjust the heat so the liquid simmers and cook, uncovered, for 5 minutes.

Spoon into serving bowls and serve with a dish of sour cream to pass at the table.

SERVE WITH: Tortilla chips and salsa.

Did You Know?

When King Henry VIII threw a dinner party, some of the delicacies of the table included grilled beaver's tail, whole roasted peacock, and boiled whale.

Choose Your Own Adventure:
HAVE A DINNER PARTY

Take your kitchen skills to the next level by cooking not just a single recipe but a whole menu and inviting your friends over. Below are 4 different menus for inspiration, but feel to mix and match or pull other recipes from the book to include. If you don't have time to make the entire menu, skip the dessert recipe and serve either fresh fruit (watermelon, grapes, and strawberries are good options), store-bought ice cream bars, or treats from a bakery.

Menu 1
- Sheet-Pan Chicken and Potatoes (page 149)
- Butter Lettuce with Green Goodness Dressing (page 93)
- Mix-in-the-Pan Applesauce Cake (page 167)

Menu 2
- Baked Mac and Cheese (page 146)
- Buttery Green Beans (page 102)
- Vanilla Cupcakes with Fudgy Frosting (page 170)

Menu 3
- Guacamole (page 140), make a double batch, with cucumber, carrots, and bell peppers for dipping

- Big Pot of Turkey Chili (page 157)
- One-Bowl Chocolate Chip Cookies (page 165)

Menu 4
- Homemade Saucy Meatballs (page 152)
- Arugula Salad with Balsamic Vinaigrette (page 91)
- Fruit Crisps in Little Jars (page 173)

10 PREP SWEETS TO EAT AND SHARE

Learning to bake before learning to cook feels a bit like eating dessert before dinner, but plenty of people I know mastered cakes and cookies before they ventured into more savory cooking. Whatever gets you excited to be in the kitchen is fine by me.

The fact is, baking is an excellent way to pick up some seriously good cooking skills, such as how to properly measure ingredients, follow a recipe, and keep tabs on what's in the oven. Without that attention to detail, baked goods don't always turn out so well.

Beyond all that, the best reason I know to do desserts is that you're often making something to share. When it comes time to celebrate a birthday, you can be the one to bake instead of buy a batch of cupcakes. And when you want to cheer up a friend, what could be better than a batch of chocolate chip cookies?

GOLDEN BANANA BREAD

A good banana bread recipe is something you should hang on to for a very long time. It's the sort of thing that tastes good (sometimes even better) a day or two after you make it. Wrap it up to give to a friend (it travels well) or keep it for yourself to eat for breakfast, as a snack, or for dessert. This one is moist, sweet, and tender. It's made with walnuts, which you can easily leave out or replace with chocolate chips. Whatever you do when you make this bread, be sure to use ripe bananas and not to mix the batter too vigorously. That will make all the difference.

Nonstick cooking spray

4 medium-size ripe bananas (they should be speckled with little brown dots)

2 eggs

⅓ cup firmly packed light or dark brown sugar

½ cup sugar

⅓ cup canola oil

¼ cup sour cream

1 teaspoon vanilla extract

1⅓ cups all-purpose flour

1 teaspoon baking soda

½ teaspoon kosher salt

½ cup chopped walnuts

KEY EQUIPMENT: loaf pan that's roughly 8½ x 4½ inches, large bowl, electric mixer, medium bowl, rubber spatula

Preheat oven to 350°F. Use nonstick cooking spray to generously grease the inside of a loaf pan.

Peel the bananas and break them up into a few pieces as you add them to a large bowl. Use an electric mixer to beat them into a gooey, thick mixture. It's okay if it's a little lumpy.

Add the eggs and beat until blended, about 30 seconds. Add the brown sugar, sugar, canola oil, sour cream, and vanilla and beat until blended and smooth, another 30 seconds or so.

Put the flour, baking soda, and salt into a separate medium bowl. Use a fork to stir everything together. With the mixer running on low speed, slowly add the flour mixture to the banana mixture and beat just until blended and you no longer see little streaks of flour. Don't mix it too much or the bread will be tough. Stir in the walnuts with a rubber spatula, just until combined.

Pour the batter into the bread pan, scraping the bottom and sides of the bowl with a rubber spatula to get every last bit.

PRO TIP: You can use this same batter to make banana muffins. Pour into greased or paper-lined muffin cups, filling them nearly to the top. Bake at 350°F until a toothpick inserted in the center comes out clean, about 18 minutes.

Bake until the bread is firm when you touch it lightly and your finger doesn't leave an indent. You can double-check for doneness by inserting a toothpick in the center. It's done when you don't see any wet batter sticking to it. This will take about 1 hour and 15 minutes.

Remove from the oven and leave the bread to cool on the counter for 20 minutes. Run a little knife around the edges of the pan and invert the bread on the counter to dislodge it. Set it upright and leave it to cool another 30 minutes before cutting.

Let Your Bananas Brown

Bananas that are slightly green or even bright yellow will certainly be sweet, but leave them a little longer to grow speckled with brown spots and they will be that much sweeter. Browned bananas may not be what you want to slice onto your cereal, but they're excellent for adding natural sweetness to breads, cakes, and breakfast smoothies

ONE-BOWL CHOCOLATE CHIP COOKIES

MAKES 2 DOZEN COOKIES

Is there anything quite so good as a homemade cookie warm from the oven? This one is crispy around the edges, chewy in the center, and oozing chocolate. A mash-up of all my favorite chocolate chip cookie recipes, it's simpler than most because you beat all the ingredients in a single bowl. Translation: less mess for the cook.

½ cup (1 stick) butter, softened to room temperature (see note)

⅔ cup firmly packed light or dark brown sugar

⅓ cup sugar

1 egg

1 teaspoon vanilla extract

1½ cups all-purpose flour

¾ teaspoon baking soda

½ teaspoon kosher salt

1½ cups semisweet or bittersweet chocolate chips

Nonstick cooking spray for greasing the baking sheets.

KEY EQUIPMENT: large bowl, electric mixer, 2 large baking sheets, spatula

Preheat oven to 325°F

Put the butter, brown sugar, and sugar in a large bowl and use an electric mixer to mix them together until smooth, about 2 minutes. Add the egg and vanilla and mix until smooth, another minute. Add the flour. Sprinkle the baking soda and salt evenly over the ingredients in the bowl. Mix on low until smooth and combined, about 30 seconds. Add chocolate chips and beat just until mixed into the dough, 5 to 10 seconds more.

Spray 2 baking sheets with nonstick cooking spray. Use a small spoon to scoop up enough dough so that it's about 1½ inches in diameter when rolled into a ball. Roll 12 balls between your palms and space them evenly over a baking sheet. Repeat with the remaining dough on the second baking sheet. You should have enough dough to make 24 cookies.

Bake until the edges of the cookies begin to turn golden brown and they no longer look raw across the top, about 10 to 12 minutes. Pull them from the oven and let cool for 5 minutes. Use a spatula to lift them from the baking sheets.

Store in a jar or cookie tin for up to 4 days.

Make Your Own Freezer Cookie Dough

Who needs Toll House when you can make your own roll of cookie dough to freeze and save for another day. Here's how: Roll any leftover cookie dough into a log that is 2 inches in diameter. Wrap it in 2 layers of plastic wrap and freeze. When you're ready to defrost and bake, just pull the dough from the freezer and leave it on the counter for 1 hour. Cut into slices and bake as instructed above. The cookies may take a little longer to cook since the dough will be cold.

Did You Know?

The chocolate chip cookie was invented during the 1930s by Ruth Wakefield at the Toll House Inn in Whitman, Massachusetts.

MIX-IN-THE-PAN APPLESAUCE CAKE

This is what's known as a *dump cake*, meaning you "dump" the ingredients into a baking pan, mix it, and pop it into the oven to bake. The result is a homey, moist cake flavored with apples, cinnamon, and brown sugar. When finished with a layer of buttery vanilla frosting, it's a favorite cake in our house. The bonus? No mixing bowls to clean up.

Cake

1¼ cups all-purpose flour

⅔ firmly packed cup brown sugar

1 teaspoon ground cinnamon

¾ teaspoon baking powder

¾ teaspoon baking soda

¼ teaspoon salt

1 egg

⅓ cup olive oil

½ cup plain Greek yogurt

½ cup unsweetened applesauce

1 teaspoon vanilla extract

(continued)

Preheat oven to 350°F.

Put the flour, brown sugar, cinnamon, baking powder, baking soda, and salt into an 8-inch square baking pan. Use a fork to thoroughly mix the ingredients together.

Use your hands to make a hole in the center of the dry ingredients. Into the hole, crack the egg and add the olive oil, yogurt, applesauce, and vanilla. Use a fork to mix the ingredients together until smooth and blended. Smooth the top of the batter with the side of a butter knife.

Bake until the cake is fairly firm when you press lightly at its center and a toothpick inserted in the middle has no wet batter sticking to it, 25 to 30 minutes.

Remove from oven and leave on the counter to cool completely before frosting, 1 hour. Leave cake in the pan.

To make the frosting, put the confectioners' sugar, butter, milk, and vanilla into a medium bowl and beat with an electric mixer until creamy and smooth. Use a butter knife to spread over the top of the cooled cake while still in the pan.

Cut into pieces and use a small spatula to lift them from the pan.

Buttercream Frosting

1½ cup confectioners' sugar

⅓ cup butter, softened to room temperature (see note on page 166)

1 tablespoon milk

½ teaspoon vanilla extract

KEY EQUIPMENT: 8-inch square baking pan, medium bowl, electric mixer, small spatula

PRO TIP: Save yourself a step and skip the frosting on the applesauce cake. It's still delicious without it and you won't have to let the cake cool before you dig in.

When Sugar Is Brown, Pack It Down

Usually when you measure a dry ingredient, such as flour, you spoon it into a measuring cup and then level it off with a knife so it's even with the edge of the cup. But when you see the words *firmly packed brown sugar* in a recipe, it means something different. In this case, you fill the measuring cup well over the top and then pack it down firmly with your hand until the sugar is level with the edge.

VANILLA CUPCAKES WITH FUDGY FROSTING

My idea of the perfect birthday cake is simple: a tender vanilla cupcake with rich chocolate frosting. I hunted around for years for just the right recipe. It eluded me until I discovered the cupcake of my dreams in the *The Kitchn Cookbook*. It's what I make for birthdays, celebrations, or when I just need a really good cupcake. My favorite part? The chocolate frosting. It will make you want to lick the bowl clean.

Cupcakes

Nonstick cooking spray (if not using paper cupcake liners)

⅓ cup butter, softened to room temperature (see note on page 166)

1 cup sugar

2 eggs

1½ cups all-purpose flour

2¼ teaspoons baking powder

½ teaspoon kosher salt

¾ cup milk

1 teaspoon vanilla extract

(continued)

Preheat oven to 350°F with the rack in the center of the oven. Line 12 muffin cups with paper liners or grease generously with nonstick cooking spray.

Put the butter and sugar in a large bowl and beat on high with an electric mixer until creamy and light, about 3 minutes. Add the eggs and continue to beat on high until creamy and blended, about 30 seconds. Add the flour and sprinkle the baking powder and salt in the bowl. Beat on low until incorporated into the batter, about 30 seconds. Add the milk and vanilla and beat on high for 3 minutes (don't worry if it's a little lumpy).

Pour the batter into the 12 muffin cups. (I find a measuring cup with a handle is a good way to scoop batter up from the bowl and pour it into the muffin cups.)

Bake the cupcakes on the center rack of the oven until done, about 20 minutes. To test for doneness, press lightly in the center of a cupcake, it shouldn't leave a dent. You can also

Fudgy Frosting

2 ounces bittersweet chocolate

½ cup heavy cream

2 tablespoons unsweetened cocoa powder

½ teaspoon vanilla extract

¼ teaspoon kosher salt

1½ to 1¾ cups confectioners' sugar

KEY EQUIPMENT: 12-cup muffin pan, 12 paper cupcake liners (optional), large bowl, electric mixer, cutting board, chef's knife, medium glass or metal bowl, small saucepan

PRO TIP: Make this as a cake instead of cupcakes by pouring the batter into a generously greased 9-inch round baking pan and baking it until done, 35 to 40 minutes. Once cool, run a knife around the edge and turn the pan over to release the cake. Turn it back over (with care so it doesn't break) and frost.

insert a toothpick into the center; it should come out clean with no wet batter.

Remove from oven and let cool on the counter completely before frosting, otherwise the heat of the cupcake will melt the frosting.

To make the frosting, put the chocolate on a cutting board and use a chef's knife to chop it into tiny pieces. Put it into a medium glass or metal bowl.

Pour the cream into a small saucepan and put on the stove over medium heat. Cook until tiny bubbles appear around the perimeter of the cream. Pour the hot cream over the chocolate, stir until they melt together, and leave it cool for 10 minutes.

Beat the chocolate and cream with an electric mixer until smooth and glossy, about 3 minutes. Add the cocoa powder, vanilla, and salt and mix until blended. Add 1½ cups confectioners' sugar and beat until thick and smooth. If the frosting looks too thin, add more confectioners' sugar, a tablespoon at a time, until it reaches the right thickness.

Use a butter knife to spread the frosting on the cooled cupcakes.

Adapted from Sara Kate Gillingham and Faith Durand. *The Kitchn Cookbook; Recipes, Kitchens & Tips to Inspire Your Cooking.* (New York: Clarkson Potter, 2014).

5 Ways to Be a Better Baker

1. **Follow the recipe.** Baking is a real science. If you tinker with a recipe too much, such as leaving out an ingredient in a cake or mixing a quick bread batter longer than instructed, you may not get the results you were hoping for. Until you are a seasoned baker, it's best to follow recipes to the letter.

2. **Double-check everything.** Once you've finished all the steps of a recipe, read it over carefully to make sure you haven't left something out. It's easy to overlook an ingredient and better to fix things before they go into the oven.

3. **Measure properly.** If you don't measure ingredients accurately it can really throw off your recipe. Use the measuring guidelines on page 9 to get it right.

4. **Do the sniff test.** A timer is essential for keeping track of baking times, but another terrific tool is your nose. Eventually, you will know just the right moment to pull a batch of cookies or a loaf of bread out of the oven simply by your sense of smell.

5. **Put love into your batter.** I don't think anyone has done a study on this, but in my experience, the best baking happens when I'm happy and putting care into what goes into my mixing bowl. Save your baking projects for when you aren't stressed or pressed for time and put love into every stir of your spoon.

FRUIT CRISPS IN LITTLE JARS

MAKES 6 SERVINGS

Assembling these Fruit Crisps in little glass jars rather than one big pan gives this old-fashioned dessert a charming update. Make them with peaches or nectarines when they're in season or use apples or pears when they're not. Serve the crisps as is or top each jar with a spoonful of vanilla or salted caramel ice cream.

6 large peaches or nectarines, or 6 medium apples or pears (no need to peel)

¼ to ⅓ cup sugar

½ cup all-purpose flour

⅓ cup rolled oats

½ cup plus 1 tablespoon packed light or dark brown sugar

6 tablespoons cold butter

KEY EQUIPMENT: Six 8-ounce glass canning jars (sold in hardware stores, cookware stores, some supermarkets, and online), paring knife, chef's knife, cutting board, medium bowl, large bowl, baking sheet

Preheat oven to 350°F.

If using peaches or nectarines, cut them in half and remove the pits. If using apples or pears, cut the fruit off the core in 4 cuts. Cut the fruit into pieces that are roughly ½-inch square until you have 4½ cups of fruit (store any leftover fruit for another use). Mix the fruit in a medium bowl with ¼ cup sugar. Taste it. If it tastes too tart, add more sugar, about 1 or 2 tablespoons. Divide fruit among the 6 jars (the fruit should be about 1 inch below the top).

Make the topping by using a fork to stir together the flour, oats, and brown sugar in a large bowl until blended. Put the butter on a cutting board and cut it lengthwise into quarters. Then cut about 8 slices across so you have many tiny cubes of butter.

Add the butter to the flour mixture, tossing it in the flour to lightly coat each cube. Pick up a piece of butter between each thumb and forefinger, press it down firmly to smash it completely. Repeat with all of the butter cubes, tossing them occasionally in the flour.

PRO TIP: If you don't want to make this in individual jars, make in an 8-inch square baking pan instead. Cut enough fruit to fill 6 cups instead of 4½ and toss with ⅓ to ½ cup sugar. Pile the fruit into the pan, sprinkle on the topping, and bake until the top is golden brown and the juices of the fruit bubble, about 40 minutes.

Once you've smashed all the butter, pick up the smashed bits, one by one, and smash them again between your thumb and fingers, and then toss again in the flour. Eventually it should look like a bowl of very coarse sand with tiny chunks of butter throughout.

Divide the topping among the jars, covering the fruit and patting it down gently.

Put the jars onto a baking sheet and bake until the juices of the fruit bubble and the top is golden brown, about 35 minutes. Serve warm or at room temperature.

How to Measure Flour

You'll have the best results if you measure flour and other dry ingredients the way I did when I developed the recipes in this book: by spooning and leveling. Here's how: Rather than plunging a measuring cup into a bag of flour, use a large spoon to scoop flour from the bag into the measuring cup. Then scrape the flat edge of a knife lightly across the top of the cup to level it before adding the flour to the mixing bowl. Easy.

Choose Your Own Adventure:
ICE CREAM BAR

It's hard to go wrong with ice cream when it comes to dessert. Skip the boring bowl of vanilla and create your own Ice Cream Bar. Set it up for ice cream sandwiches, sundaes, creative cones, or go big and do all three.

ICE CREAM
vanilla, chocolate, chocolate chip, coffee, strawberry

MAKE AN ICE CREAM SANDWICH	or	MAKE AN ICE CREAM SUNDAE	or	MAKE AN ICE CREAM CONE

MAKE AN ICE CREAM SANDWICH

put 1 scoop between 2 cookies
- Chocolate Chip Cookies (page 165)
- oatmeal cookies
- gingersnaps
- graham crackers

roll edges in
- chopped peanuts
- sliced almonds
- toasted coconut
- mini chocolate chips

or

MAKE AN ICE CREAM SUNDAE

drizzle 1 to 2 scoops with
- fudge sauce
- butterscotch sauce
- melted raspberry jam
- pure maple syrup

top with
- chopped walnuts
- favorite berries
- chocolate chips
- whipped cream

or

MAKE AN ICE CREAM CONE

put 1 to 2 scoops on a
- sugar cone
- waffle cone
- wafer cone

roll cone in
- chopped peanuts
- chocolate sprinkles
- crushed pretzels
- shredded coconut

ACKNOWLEDGMENTS

This book began as a post on my blog about the cooking chops that kids need before they head off into the world. It's a topic about which I care enormously and one that my readers really responded to, so much so that it prompted me to turn an 800-word story into a full-blown book. I'm grateful to the Mom's Kitchen Handbook community for planting the seed.

First and foremost, I want to thank my girls: Isabelle, Rosie, and Virginia. I don't know that I could write a book for teenagers without having three of my own. Your strong opinions, discerning palates, and insights are reflected on every page of this book. I love you ladies beyond comprehension. And to my husband, Joe: You tolerate the constant rattle of pots and pans, whir of the blender, and never-ending pile of dishes at the sink with such patience. Your seemingly endless supply of love and support astounds me. I'm so grateful.

To my parents, siblings, and beloved tribe of friends: thank you for listening, caring, and loving me and my work.

To my earnest and thoughtful team of teenage recipe testers: It was so enlightening to see how you responded to the recipes I sent your way. Thank you, Will Donahue, Sofia Ghilzai Morris, Grace Banfield, Luca Perr, Emmy Etlin, Sean Hart, April Hart, and Jackie Carlson. And a special shout-out to Sarah Stadlin for your hard work in the kitchen.

I can't say thank you enough to Spring Utting (and Astrid and Sasha, too), for your enthusiasm for my recipes and invaluable feedback. And to all of the other friends and family who listened, edited, and pitched in with testing: Sally Kuzemchak, Sarah Copeland, Heather Prime, Heather Wall, Nina Denigris, Charlotte Prime, Pilar Prime, Suzanne Bergeron, Nikki Pearl, Mark Sullivan, Annie Sullivan Cobb, Alison Sullivan, and Pam Rupright.

Much gratitude to photographer Alanna Taylor-Tobin for bringing my recipes to life and teaching me to be a better food stylist along the way.

Thank you to my incomparable agent, Carole Bidnick, for ferrying this book along and always being at the other end of the phone line or computer keyboard. You really are the best.

Last but not least, I am grateful for Jennifer Urban-Brown and Sara Bercholz at Roost Books for believing in this project and working with me to bring my vision to the page.

RESOURCES

Even the most seasoned cook doesn't go it alone in the kitchen. Below you'll find recommended resources to help you along your journey at the stove.

STARTER COOKBOOKS

Bittman, Mark. *How to Cook Everything: 2,000 Simple Recipes for Great Food.* New York: Wiley, 2011.

López-Alt, J. Kenji. *The Food Lab: Better Home Cooking through Science.* New York: W.W. Norton, 2015.

Luchetti, Emily, and Lisa Weiss. *The Fearless Baker.* New York: Little, Brown and Company, 2011.

Nosrat, Samin. *Salt, Fat, Acid, Heat: Mastering the Elements of Good Cooking.* New York: Simon & Schuster, 2017.

Peternell, Cal. *12 Recipes.* New York: Morrow Cookbooks, 2014.

Turshen, Julia. *Small Victories: Recipes, Advice + Hundreds of Ideas for Home-Cooking Triumphs.* San Francisco: Chronicle Books, 2016.

WEBSITES/BLOGS

BBC Good Food | bbcgoodfood.com

Epicurious | epicurious.com

Eating Well | eatingwell.com

The Kitchn | thekitchn.com

Minimalist Baker | minimalistbaker.com

Serious Eats | seriouseats.com

Smitten Kitchen | smittenkitchen.com

What's Gaby Cooking | whatsgabycooking.com

Nutrition Stripped | nutritionstripped.com

COOKWARE

Here are some ideas for where to find kitchen equipment, ranging from top-of the-line luxury stores to places you might find cooking tools for free.

High End	Bargain	Online	Free
Williams-Sonoma	Ross	Amazon.com	Swiped from your parent's kitchen
Sur La Table	T.J. Maxx	Overstock.com	
Bloomingdales	Marshalls	**Secondhand**	
	Restaurant supply stores	Garage sales	
		Flea markets	

INDEX

ABOUT THE AUTHOR

Katie Sullivan Morford is a writer and registered dietitian with a master's degree in nutrition from New York University. She is the author of two cookbooks, *Rise & Shine* (Roost Books, 2016) and *Best Lunch Box Ever* (Chronicle Books, 2013), which was nominated for an IACP award for best family cookbook. Her work has been featured in a number of publications, including *Family Circle, O: The Oprah Magazine, Real Simple, Parents, Cooking Light,* the *San Francisco Chronicle*, and the *New York Times*. She is also the voice behind the popular blog *Mom's Kitchen Handbook*. Katie is a firm believer in empowering young people in the kitchen and over the years has taught cooking and nutrition to kids of every age. Her experience raising her own children at the stove, all of whom are now teenagers and college students, prompted her to write this book. Katie lives in San Francisco with her husband, three daughters, and one very small dog.